Wu Ming

presents

mped below

Thomas Müntze

This essential new series features classic texts by key figures that took centre stage during a period of insurrection. Each book is introduced by a major contemporary radical writer who shows how these incendiary words still have the power to inspire, to provoke and maybe to ignite new revolutions . . .

Also available:

Sheila Rowbotham presents Mary Wollstonecraft:
A Vindication of the Rights of Woman

Hugo Chávez presents Simón Bolívar:
The Bolívarian Revolution

Dr Jean-Bertrand Aristide presents Toussaint L'Ouverture:
The Haitian Revolution

Slavoj Žižek presents Trotsky:
Terrorism and Communism

Michael Hardt presents Thomas Jefferson:
The Declaration of Independence

Slavoj Žižek presents Mao:
On Practice and Contradiction

Walden Bello presents Ho Chi Minh:
Down with Colonialism!

Alain Badiou presents Marx:
The Civil War in France

Tariq Ali present Castro:
The Declarations of Havana

Slavoj Žižek presents Robespierre:
Virtue and Terror

Terry Eagleton presents Jesus Christ:
The Gospels

Geoffrey Robertson presents The Levellers:
The Putney Debates

WU MING PRESENTS

THOMAS MÜNTZER

———————◆———————

SERMON TO THE PRINCES

WITH A PREFACE AND ANNOTATIONS BY
ALBERTO TOSCANO

Translated by Michael G. Baylor

VERSO

London • New York

The works of Thomas Müntzer collected here were first
published in this translation as *Revelation and Revolution: The Basic
Writings of Thomas Müntzer* by Associated University Press 1993

This edition first published by Verso 2010
Translated by Michael G. Baylor
Introduction © Wu Ming
Preface © Alberto Toscano
© editorial matter Verso 2010
All rights reserved

1 3 5 7 9 10 8 6 4 2

Verso
UK: 6 Meard Street, London W1F 0EG
US: 20 Jay Street, Suite 1010, Brooklyn, NY 11201
www.versobooks.com

ISBN: 978-1-84467-320-9

British Library Cataloguing in Publication Data
A catalogue record for this book is available from the British Library

Library of Congress Cataloging-in-Publication Data
A catalog record for this book is available from the Library of Congress

Typeset in Bembo by Hewer Text UK Ltd, Edinburgh
Printed in the US by Worldcolor/Fairfield

Contents

Preface

The Resurrections of Thomas Müntzer

Alberto Toscano

My seed did not fall on stony ground. Now it is growing.
Now it will bear fruit. You will overcome.
> – Thomas Müntzer, in Berta Lask's play,
> *Thomas Müntzer. Dramatisches Gemälde
> des Deutschen Bauernkrieges von 1525*

In the eyes of the German working-classes, Müntzer was and
is the most brilliant embodiment of heretical communism.
> – Karl Kautsky, *Communism in Central
> Europe in the Time of the Reformation*

'Anno domini 1525, at the beginning of the year, there was a
great, unprecedented upheaval of the Common Man throughout the German lands' – thus wrote a contemporary of what
has come to be known as the German Peasants' War. More
than three hundred years later, in 'On the Jewish Question',
Karl Marx referred to the events of 1524–6 as 'the most radical
fact of German history'. Fusing together theological extremism
with the conflicts that stemmed from profound economic trans-
formations and the exactions of the German princes, the Peasants' War was not only the most notable revolt 'from below' in
Europe prior to the French Revolution (with around 100,000

peasants killed in its suppression), it also became a *locus classicus* for those who wished to meditate on the bonds between religious activism and social upheaval, and to explore the volatile combination of theological innovation and political strategy.

Despite the presence of other eloquent leaders and agitators within the widespread movement of revolt (Michael Gaismair in Tyrol, for instance), it is Thomas Müntzer who is often singled out as the emblematic figure in the Peasants' War; as Ernst Bloch would have it, he was 'the theologian of the revolution'. The reception of Müntzer has been divided, to say the least. In intellectual portraits and narratives almost invariably skewed by the political passions or aversions of their authors, this self-described 'servant of God against the godless' has featured either as a dangerous fanatic, or as a heroic revolutionary precursor.

The idea of the *Schwärmer*, or fanatic, as the utmost threat to the orderly reproduction of society, the one who collapses the City of God into the City of Man in an apocalyptic conflagration – an idea that has since exercised a powerful hold on Western political thought – can indeed be traced back to the early responses to Müntzer by the Wittenberg reformers, and in particular by his erstwhile interlocutors Luther and Melanchthon. After their break around 1523, brought on by Müntzer's increasingly overt political agitation and his related repudiation of key tenets of Luther's Protestantism – above all the 'Pauline' justification of obedience to earthly authorities – Luther, adamant to demarcate his own project of reformation from Müntzer's subversive preaching and to quell an anti-authoritarian and iconoclastic surge that could be laid at his door, lambasted 'the Satan of Allstedt' as fanatical, seditious and demagogical. In the 1524 *Letter to the Princes of Saxony Concerning the Seditious Spirit*, Luther castigated Müntzer's doctrine of the primacy of spirit over the letter, and what he (correctly) perceived as its revolutionary implications: that it would lead the common people 'to overthrow civil authority and make themselves lords of the world', thereby besmirching a faith which fought against papal authority in order to purify itself *from* authority, not so as to overturn it. The 'villainous and blood-thirsty prophet', Müntzer, aimed at imposing faith by the sword, and drawing from the scriptures a principle of violence. Luther insisted that the Gospels could not be used to justify this mutinous meddling in worldly things.

And yet the ban on political revolt (the greatest evil and impediment to salvation), joined with the legitimation of the authorities that ruled over the fallen world, meant that Luther, far from condemning violence as such, extolled it when it referred to the suppression of the false prophet and his plebeian followers. In May 1525, in a screed written prior to, but published in the wake of, the peasant armies' bloody rout at Frankenhausen – *Against the Robbing and Murdering Hordes of Peasants* – Luther applied the full power of his pen to singing the praises of the princes' swords. In a text that could serve as the template for the many justifications of untrammelled, fanatical violence against 'fanatics' in the centuries that followed, he wrote:

> Let whoever can stab, smite, slay. If you die in doing it, good for you! A more blessed death can never be yours, for you die while obeying the divine word and commandment in Romans 13, and in loving service of your neighbour, whom you are rescuing from the bonds of hell and of the devil. ... If anyone thinks this is too harsh, let him remember that rebellion is intolerable and that the destruction of the world is to be expected every hour.

Though none of Müntzer's many detractors throughout the ages ever reached the pitch of Luther's vituperations, the theme of Müntzer as fanatic is endemic. Philipp Melanchthon, who had befriended Müntzer in the latter's early passage through Wittenberg, would later go on – in the anonymously published *History of Thomas Müntzer, the author of the Thuringian revolt, very profitable reading* – to justify the bloody repression meted out against the 'rabble' and its devil-possessed false prophet. In his commentary to Aristotle's *Politics* (1529), he would then enshrine the notion of the fanatic in political theory, condemning as 'fanatical people' those whom, like Müntzer and his comrades, choose to condemn private property on the basis of the Gospels and thus lay waste to the principles of 'civil society'.

Müntzer's fanatical fame rests in part on his penchant for rhetorical assaults of arresting violence (which shouldn't blind us to the full range of his writing, from pastoral letters to scriptural exegesis, dream interpretations to liturgy). In his letter to his arch-nemesis, Count Ernst von Mansfeld, Müntzer writes: 'Just tell us, you miserable sack of worms, who made you a prince over the people whom God redeemed with his dear blood?' He warns the common people that the priests 'will shit on you with a new logic, twisting the word of God'. His violent exhortations range from the allegorical – 'The living God is sharpening his scythe in me, so that later I can cut down the red poppies and the blue cornflowers' – to the frenzied, as in his letter to the people of Allstedt:

> At them, at them, while the fire is hot! Do not let your sword get cold, do not let your arms go lame! Strike – cling, clang! – on the anvils of Nimrod. Throw their towers to the ground! As long as [the godless] live, it is not possible for you to be emptied of human fear. You cannot be told about God as long as they rule over you. At them, at them, while you have daylight! God leads you – follow, follow!

His enemies – Luther, the 'godless', the priests and princes – were the object of a rich panoply of insults: 'abandoned reprobates', 'thin-shitters', 'platelickers', 'clownish, testicled doctors', 'toadspawn', 'whore-riders'. As though his confirmed statements did not suffice, Melanchthon's *History* even puts the following declamation in his mouth, as if to seal the accusation of fanatical desecration and false prophecy: 'I shit on God if he does not do my bidding.' In the image and the reality of Müntzer, scatology and eschatology are never too far apart.

The image of Müntzer as the fanatic, transmitted in plays and chronicles, as well as in his portraits – which, as Goertz's fine biography shows, were based not on observation but on a kind of physiognomy of heresy – still exerted its fascination well into the twentieth century. Thus G. R. Elton, in his *Reformation Europe 1517–1559*, memorably introduces Müntzer as a 'youngish man full of violent hatred for all things other than they should have been, university trained, an idealist of the kind familiar in all revolutions', dubs him 'the demonic genius of the early Reformation' and concludes, in terms wholly congruent with the tradition initiated by Luther and Melanchthon, that he was 'not so much a constructive revolutionary as an unrestrained fanatic, and in his preaching of violence a dangerous lunatic'. But the most influential depiction of Müntzer as a fanatic is to be found in Norman Cohn's classic *The Pursuit of the Millennium*, a text that, like so many others on Müntzer, posits a short circuit between the distant past of the Peasants' War and the political exigencies of the present (in Cohn's case taking the form of Cold War anti-communism). For Cohn, 'Müntzer was a *propheta* obsessed by eschatological phantasies which he attempted to translate into reality by exploiting social discontent.' His narrative of the theologian of the revolution, albeit driven by the need to condemn political fanaticism, often attains a quasi-cinematic effect, as when he writes: 'Obsessed as always by the impending destruction of the ungodly, he had a red crucifix and a naked sword carried in front of him when, at the head of an armed band, he patrolled the streets of the town.' Cohn's ultimate thesis, for which Müntzer plays a pivotal and emblematic role, remains very influential to this very day. He argues, in a nutshell, that the 'totalitarianisms' (Communism and

Fascism) were the bearers of archaic 'phantasies' belonging to the 'popular apocalyptic lore of Europe'.

This verdict represents the conscious reversal of a communist and Marxist tradition that adopted Müntzer as a heroic herald of egalitarian, revolutionary politics, precariously poised between a decaying mediaeval world rife with urges for pre-capitalist communism and the class struggle within and against a rising capitalist society. This tradition, which views Müntzer as the fiery precursor of contemporary revolutions, has generally downplayed the apocalyptic and mystical thrust of Müntzer's sermons and texts, as well as his theological and scriptural originality. It focuses instead on his capacity to crystallize the discontent of the peasants and the 'common man', which eventually led to organizing their revolt. It is significant in this respect to note that the 'resurrections' of Thomas Müntzer (to adopt a notion recently proposed by Alain Badiou) have frequently coincided with upsurges of revolutionary struggle. Thus the first proper biography of Müntzer, by Ströbel, was written in the wake of the French Revolution, while Zimmerman, the author of the influential *General History of the Peasants' Revolt*, was a Young Hegelian who sought to read Müntzer through the radical democratic struggles of Germany in the 1840s. Engels, in his seminal text, *The Peasant War in Germany* (1850), turned to Müntzer in order to think through the defeat of the 1848 revolutions and to 'resurrect' a fitting, if anachronistic, revolutionary emblem. Müntzer also returned with the defeated German revolution of 1917–23, in Ernst Bloch's *Thomas Müntzer: Theologian of the Revolution*, and in more popular modes, such as Berta Lask's agitprop play, staged in 1925 in Eisleben for 'Red Müntzer Day'. Not to forget the resurgent interest in this communist precursor among the Situationists around 1968, or his rediscovery by Luther Blissett and Wu Ming in a political short circuit with Zapatismo and the alter-globalization movement. All of these moments saw the revitalization of a communist principle which was famously extorted from Müntzer under torture, shortly before his execution:

> 'All property should be held in common' (*Omnia sunt communia*) and should be distributed to each according to his needs, as the occasion required. Any prince, count, or lord who did not want to do this, after first being warned about it, should be beheaded or hanged.

The matrix for the recovery of Müntzer as a revolutionary icon – an icon of egalitarian iconoclasm, of the battle against what he called 'dead wooden things' – was and remains Engels's powerful text. Indeed, the importance of the figure of Müntzer for Engels exceeds the simple evaluation of the Peasants' War, profoundly colouring the Marxist understanding of revolutions and revolts which find their symbolism and legitimation in religious or theological conceptions of the world. Three basic elements underlie Engels's critical history: the idea of Müntzer as the representative of a class and of its political direction; the understanding of Müntzer's apocalyptic theology as an intractable limitation of a political project ahead of its time; the attention to Müntzer as a savvy revolutionary agitator and strategist. Engels presents a tripartite schema in which three 'camps' confront one another: 'the conservative Catholic camp' of the defenders of the status quo (imperial authorities, some princes, nobility, etc.), 'the camp of *burgher-like moderate Lutheran* reforms' (lesser nobility, burghers, some lay princes) and the '*revolutionary* party' of plebeians and peasants, of which Müntzer is the most eloquent spokesperson. Importantly, it is the plebeians, among which one would count the Mansfeld miners and poorer townspeople who Müntzer strove to organize, and not the peasants, who represent the crucial class for Engels, 'the only class that stood outside the existing official society'. Müntzer's restless organizational activity – his sermons, letters, constant peregrinations, flights and agitation, as well as his later armed endeavours – would then be aimed at fomenting the unity of this 'class', building alliances among its disparate members and with the peasantry in the broader 'party' of revolution. Political organizations, such as the 'League of the Elect' in Allstedt, or the 'Eternal Council' and revolutionary commune in Mühlhausen, would be aimed at this purpose. (The greatest contribution of Karl Kautsky's treatment of Müntzer in his 1897 *Communism in Central Europe* lies precisely in following the red thread of this organizational activity.)

Where it comes to the theological dimension of Müntzer's thought, Engels presents Müntzer's religious language variously as a 'screen', a 'flag' or a 'mask' for his underlying revolutionary class politics. Though this theme is familiar enough, the reasons adduced for it are worth reflecting on. Müntzer's camp, the 'plebeians', were both the 'symptoms' of a decaying feudalism and the 'first precursors of modern bourgeois society'. Along with their spiritual and political leader, they were compelled by this situation of transition into a theological, or even apocalyptic, acceleration, with the ideological effects that this entailed. Engels's explanation is worth quoting at length. The fact that they were both symptoms and precursors

> explains why the plebeian opposition even then could not confine itself to fighting only feudalism and the privileged burghers; why, in fantasy at least, it reached beyond the then scarcely dawning modern bourgeois society, why, an absolutely propertyless group, it questioned the institutions, views and conceptions common to all societies based on class antagonisms. In this respect, the chiliastic dream-visions of early Christianity offered a very convenient starting-point. On the other hand, this sally beyond both the present and even the future could be nothing but violent and fantastic, and of necessity fell back into the narrow limits set by the contemporary situation.

What's more, the cunning of capitalist history meant that the 'anticipation of communism by fantasy became in reality an anticipation of modern bourgeois conditions', as 'vague Christian equality' turned into 'equality before the law', and so on. This verdict of the necessary failure of this humanist and millenarian revolution was partly seconded by Guy Debord, in his refutation of Cohn's argument in *The Society of the Spectacle*:

> Millenarianism – revolutionary class struggle speaking the language of religion for the last time – [...] is already a modern revolutionary tendency that as yet lacks *the consciousness that it is only historical*. The millenarians had to lose because they could not recognize the revolution as their own operation.

Prior to the more recent re-evaluations of Müntzer by the likes of Goertz and the Italian scholar Tommaso La Rocca, it was perhaps only Ernst Bloch – in his 1921 *Thomas Müntzer: Theologian of the Revolution* – who tried to do justice to the interweaving of apocalyptic theology, mystical spirituality and revolutionary politics in Müntzer. Bloch does not see the theological impetus of the 'revolution of the common man' of 1525 as the mere index of socio-economic immaturity. On the contrary, he views it as one of those situations that bears witness to the fact that 'the superstructure is often in advance of an ... economy that will only later attain its maturity'. In other words, unlike his great critic on this point, Georg Lukács, Bloch wants to stress the anticipatory character of Müntzer's anachronism, without immediately relegating it to the scrapheap of necessary failures. What's more, rather than a screen or a mask, Müntzer's theology – with its emphasis on the primacy of the spirit and necessity of suffering, its injunction that the believer make himself empty and detach himself from the world, but also its strong emphasis on the coming deification of man in the millennium – is for Bloch a potent

driving force for his political agitation. Rather than accepting the disjunction between (premature) political content and
(sterile) religious form, Bloch finds in Müntzer the paradoxical
union of theology and revolution, without the one serving
as an instrument for the other. Joining the 'absolute natural
right' of a millenarian Christianity (theocracy *qua* equality) to
a very strategic grasp of social forces and political forms (the
alliance with the miners and the formation of the League of
the Elect), Bloch's Müntzer combines '*the most efficacious at the
real level and the most efficacious at the surreal level* and puts them
both at the summit of the same revolution'. Thus, where the
imminent Apocalypse was for Luther an element in the justification of worldly authorities, for Müntzer – as demonstrated
by his gripping and hallucinatory interpretation of the Book of
Daniel in the *Sermon to the Princes* – it is more reason to acceler-
ate and intensify the struggle for a community of equals, where
the fear of God would not be impeded by the fear for the
authorities, where it would be possible for the poor (and even
the 'heathens': Müntzer makes some interesting remarks about
the superfluity of scripture and confession for true belief) to
embrace a Christian life without the depredations of the 'godless' (a 'sociological' category, as La Rocca has usefully pointed
out, which includes the clergy and authorities that stand in the
way of a religion of the common man).

More recently, Hans-Jürgen Goertz has pointed out how for
Müntzer – contrary to the doctrine of the two cities and the
Lutheran separation of church and state – the transformation
of the inner or spiritual order of man, a mystical theme drawn
from his reading of Tauler and others, is inseparable from the
transformation of the outer order. For Müntzer, writes Goertz,
the issue 'really was one of a transformation of relationships,
namely those binding individuals to God, to themselves and to
the church and temporal authorities to God and people'. Thus,
the 'revolution in consciousness is a political and social revo-

lution'. And this revolution, which is inseparable in its very grammar from the thematic of apocalypse, of 'a momentous, invincible, future reformation' (*Sermon to the Princes*), is driven throughout by a rejection of the very idea that any worldly authority, especially ones embroiled in the exploitation of the common people, should ever inspire fear or be immune from insurrection, if its rule is unjust and exploitative. As Müntzer retorts to 'the unspiritual soft-living Flesh at Wittenberg' (i.e., Luther) in *Highly Provoked Defence*, were he to be judged by someone who neither 'loved insurrection' nor was 'averse to a justified uprising', it would be evident that it is not a mere desire to trigger a revolt that has spurred his agitation among the miners and their ilk, but the belief that 'the power of the sword as well as the key to realise sins is in the hands of the whole community'. In a passage of *Highly Provoked Defence* that exemplifies the scriptural vitriol and political energy of his writing, this critique of the Lutheran justification of authority is combined with an attack on the kind of economic oppression that the princes' 'sword' (and Luther's theology) makes possible:

> Behold, the basic source of usury, theft, and robbery is our lords and princes, who take all creatures for their private property. The fish in the water, the birds in the air, the animals of the earth must all be their property, Isaiah 5[:8]. And then they let God's commandment go forth among the poor and they say, 'God has commanded, "Thou shalt not steal".' But this commandment does not apply to them since they oppress all men – the poor peasant, the artisan, and all who live are flayed and sheared, Micah 3[:2f.]. But, as soon as anyone steals the smallest thing, he must hang. And to this Doctor Liar says, 'Amen.' The lords themselves are responsible for making the poor people their enemy. They do not want to remove the cause of insurrection, so how, in the long

run, can things improve? I say this openly, so Luther asserts I must be rebellious. So be it!

This call to undo the iniquitous pact between the 'sword' of sovereignty and the flaying and fleecing of the creatures and the poor was resurrected in 1789, 1848, 1919, 1968, and many other, less familiar dates. 'Red Müntzer days' may still lie ahead. Whether they will be breathtaking anticipations or doomed anachronisms remains to be seen.

Introduction

Spectres of Müntzer at Sunrise / Greeting the 21st Century

Wu Ming

. . . A few months before the summit we started to write epic texts such as *From the Multitudes of Europe...* (and many more), you know, it was like an edict and it went: 'We are the peasants of the Jacquerie... We are the thirty-four thousand men that answered the call of Hans the Piper... We are the serfs, miners, fugitives, and deserters that joined Pugachev's Cossacks to overthrow the autocracy of Russia...' Then we pulled media stunts in order to create expectations for Genoa. An example: on a quiet springtime night, we put placards around the necks of the most visible statues in Bologna (guys like Garibaldi and other nineteenth-century national heroes), with messages encouraging all citizens to go to Genoa [...] We wanted to persuade as many people as possible to go to Genoa, and we ended up convincing as many people as possible to fall into a full-scale police ambush. Demonstrators were assaulted, beaten to a bloody pulp, arrested, even tortured. We didn't expect such mayhem. Nobody did. I regret we were so naïve and caught off-guard, although I think that was a crucial moment for the latest generation of activists. In a way, it was important to be there. That

experience has created bonds between a transnational multitude of human beings […] We'll see the consequences of
that 'being there' for a long time to come, on a grass roots,
extended, long-tailed level.

– Wu Ming interviewed by Robert P. Baird,
Chicago Review 52:2/3/4, October 2006

0. A PRESENT FROM THE MONKEYS

It happened one chilly night of March 2001.

It happened in Nurio, state of Michoacán, Mexico, where all
the indigenous tribes of the country were gathered to demand
an Indian Rights Act. It was the third meeting of the National
Indian Congress, largely a creation of the Zapatistas, those
media-savvy poetic warriors who had seemingly appeared out
of nowhere – out of the depths of time – seven years before.
U2 were wrong, sometimes something changes on New Year's
Day. Sometimes an army of balaclava-wearing Mayan peasants occupy a city and get their message across to millions of
people. It occurred in San Cristóbal de las Casas, state of Chiapas, Mexico, on January 1, 1994.

And there we were, seven years later, in the darkness on
the edge of Nurio. The Zapatistas were there, Subcomandante
Marcos was there, for the indigenous meeting took place during
the famous March of Dignity.

The March: throngs of people travelling on battered coaches
covered thousands of miles, from the backwoods of Chiapas
to the spectacularly crowded Zócalo, the biggest square in
Mexico City. Twenty days of travel, twenty days of poetry
delivered by Marcos in seven allegorical speeches called the
'Seven Keys'.

Nurio was a stop on that journey, and we, the Wu Ming
collective, were there, at least some of us. Marcos and the Zap-

atistas were accompanied by people from all parts of the world, a multifarious procession of journalists, activists, intellectuals, artists and parasites. We'd come all the way from Italy as members of a bizarre delegation the locals called '*los monos blancos*', the white monkeys. That was a pun, as '*mono*' is also Spanish for 'overalls'. Back at home, we were usually called '*le tute bianche*', the white overalls. In a strange semantic twist, a work garment had temporarily become a symbol of civil disobedience, and many people wore overalls at demonstrations. We kept them on for the whole march, and they ceased being white long before we arrived in Mexico City. There was never any occasion for taking a bath; we were quite filthy.

Sometimes the intent in calling us 'monkeys' was derogatory and xenophobic, especially in the reactionary press, but we adopted the name ourselves and later wrote an allegorical little story, *The Fable of the White Monkey*, which started like this:

After many years Don Durito, the black beetle, decided to leave the forest. He called on all animals near and far, even those from beyond the sea, so they could accompany him to the city. Many beasts came down from the mountains, others came through the sea. The strangest one was a white monkey from a very far land. Her colour was in stark contrast with the colours of the earth, and she looked very odd. The other animals were amazed looking at her. Every day the white monkey plodded along on a hard ground, under a sunshine that her skin had never experienced. She was awkward and clumsy, but did anything she could to be helpful and prove that she wasn't out of place. Many times she arrived late at the scheduled stops, but she never failed to show up.

We looked like beggars, and yet – as is sometimes the case with beggars – there must have been something interesting about our ways, since the commanders of the Zapatista Army appointed us as their bodyguards. No kidding. At a certain point during the march, we, the Italian *monos blancos*, became the commanders' security service. And what a sight we made!

It was mostly performance art, more appearance than substance. Who knows what Marcos and the others had in mind when they chose us. Maybe they just wanted to pull a prank. Luckily, we didn't put on airs. (Well, at least not all the time.) And even if we had put on airs, the steady flow of insults from the reactionary media – and even president Vicente Fox himself – would have reminded us that we were dirty, raggedy, awkward, odd-looking monkeys.

You're not familiar with this river – Don Durito told the strange animal – but you've got big strong hands. You'll build the bridge to the other bank. The white monkey, thrilled by such responsibility, started to work with a will. She worked day and night, in the sun and the rain. In the meanwhile, the slanderous fox was spreading lies about her among the other beasts, and the parrots kept saying: – She isn't one of us. She doesn't belong here, she's got another colour. Don't trust her, the bridge she's building will collapse and you will drown!

The bear, the coyote, the black monkey and all the earth-coloured animals watched the monkey working and discussed among themselves:

– She comes from far away, but she's our friend. She's working so we can cross the river.

– But this isn't her river. We don't know who she really is, we can't trust her.

Then old Don Felix, the eagle that could see everything, said that Don Durito had assigned the task to the foreigner precisely because she was different and came from afar. For that reason, her work would have a greater meaning for all.

At last we reached Mexico City and basked in the reflected light of the Zapatistas. A correspondent from the left-wing daily paper *La Jornada* wrote:

> On Saturday, March 11th, during the walk from Xochimilco to the Zócalo, the Italian monos blancos who escorted the Zapatista caravan caught a glimpse of a placard, one of the many the crowd used to communicate with the general command of the Zapatista army. That placard said: 'THE WHITE MONKEYS HAVE BALLS'. It was meant as a compensation for all the insults and smears which, in the previous days, had turned these Europeans into targets of a xenophobic campaign.

But let's go back to that cold night in Nurio. What happened in that bivouac on Mexico's central plateau? What happened that was so special?

Well, nothing much. Just a tiny gesture. While some campers were lighting the bonfire, one of us approached the Subcomandante and gave him a copy of our novel *Q*, which we'd written under the name 'Luther Blissett'. It was a copy of the Spanish-language edition. On the title page was a dedication:

> For 'El Sub'
> as the struggle keeps us warm in a cold night,
> from a *mono blanco* (now of all the colours of the earth)
> who happens to be the author.

Marcos read those lines and looked stunned: – You're the author? And you're a *mono blanco*?

– Yes, I am. I wrote it together with three other guys, and they're *monos blancos* too.

He thanked our comrade, took the book and walked away.

When the bridge was half-built, Don Durito gathered all the animals on the bank of the river.

After that, he told the white monkey to go to the window, so everyone could see her. Then he addressed the animals and said: – She is building a good bridge, but she can't finish it alone. Nobody could do it without help.

The white monkey got puzzled and asked: – Then why did you put me to work alone?

Don Durito closed the window and allowed the white monkey to look in the glass. She stared at the reflected image and hardly recognized herself.

Her coat wasn't white anymore. Now it was of all the colours of the earth.

I. MARCOS, MÜNTZER AND *Q* (1994–99)

'[...] I fought [...] alongside men who really thought they would put an end to injustice and wickedness on earth. There were thousands of us, we were an army. Our hope was shattered on the plain at Frankenhausen, on the fifteenth of May 1525. Then I abandoned a man to his fate, to the weapons of the lansquenets. I carried with me his bag full of letters, names and hopes. And the suspicion of having been betrayed, sold to the forces of the princes like a herd at a market.' It's still hard to utter the name. 'That man was Thomas Müntzer.'

I can't see him, but I sense his astonishment, perhaps the incredulity of someone who thinks he's talking to a ghost.

His voice is practically a whisper. 'You really fought with Thomas Müntzer?'

– Luther Blissett, *Q*

To this day, we don't know if Marcos ever had a chance to read the book. He's been supernaturally busy since then, and the situation in Chiapas (indeed, in all of Mexico) seems to have worsened considerably. However, the gift had a precise meaning for us: it symbolized the completion of a cycle, from the sixteenth-century Peasants' War (the subject of the novel) to the Zapatista *Levantamiento* (Uprising).

The Peasants' War was the biggest popular revolt of its time. It broke out at the heart of the Holy Roman Empire and was savagely repressed in 1525, one year before the Spanish conquistadores began their bloody invasion of southern Mexico which destroyed the Mayan civilization.

The Zapatista Levantamiento was the most inspiring peasant rebellion of our time. It began in southern Mexico on the initiative of Mayan activists and has had an influence on radical social conflict all across today's unholy empire.

Call it a chiasmus if you like.

The Peasants' War was a prefiguring event, in the same way its main agitator, Thomas Müntzer, was a prefiguring character. It was literally a *pre*-figuration because the social order that Müntzer and the revolutionary peasants envisioned was far ahead of their time; indeed, it's still ahead of *our* time. Yet it wasn't just a collective hallucination accompanied by bursts of mass violence. That's the conservative interpretation started by Martin Luther and refined by Norman Cohn, who described Müntzer as a forerunner of modern-day totalitarianism and Nazi madness. Bullshit. The peasants were far from crazy. They had social programmes (albeit crude ones) and concrete goals to achieve. Their needs were real and their political practices were rooted in the social reality of their time. Their achievements were tangible: towns were conquered, revolutionary councils were established and the power structure was shaken from the foundations up to the princes' rotting teeth. In a feudal territory fragmented into countless city-states, the Peasants' War was a boundless, national, pan-Germanic rebellion long before Germany came to exist as a nation. The peasants' mistakes – both ideological and strategical – were immanent in that socio-historical context, but their politics had started to transcend it. They were defeated and massacred, but their legacy is still with us, buried in the ground beneath our feet, and it threatens to resurface every time the social order is challenged from the bottom up. As for the peasant leaders' rhetoric, it still resounds throughout the centuries.[1] In many ways and through many voices, Müntzer still speaks to us.

He certainly spoke to four countercultural activists at the end of 1995, two years after the news of the Levantamiento had crossed the Atlantic, inspiring a new phenomenon called the Luther Blissett Project.

> In the early/mid Nineties the 'Luther Blissett' collective identity was created and adopted by an informal network of people (artists, hackers, and activists) interested in using the power of myths, and moving beyond agit-prop 'counter-information'. In Bologna, my circle of friends shared an obsession with the eternal return of such archetypal figures as folk heroes and tricksters. We spent our days exploring pop culture, studying the language of the Mexican Zapatistas, collecting stories of media hoaxes and communication guerrilla warfare since the 1920's (Berlin Dada stuff, futuristic soirées etc.), obsessively re-watching one particular movie, *Slap Shot* by George Roy Hill, starring Paul Newman as hockey player Reggie Dunlop. We liked Reggie Dunlop very much, he was the perfect trickster, the Anansi of African legends, the Coyote of Native American legends, Ulysses manipulating the cyclop's mind.
>
> What if we could build our own 'Reggie Dunlop', a 'trickster with a thousand faces', a golem made of the clay of three rivers – the agit-prop tradition, folk mythology, and pop culture? What if we started a completely new

role play game, using all the media platforms available at the time to spread the legend of a new folk hero, a hero fueled-up by collective intelligence?

– Henry Jenkins III, 'How *Slapshot* Inspired
a Cultural Revolution: An Interview with
the Wu Ming Foundation', Confessions
of an Aca/Fan weblog, October 2006

The communication strategies of the Zapatistas were a big influence on the Luther Blissett Project. References to El Sub and the EZLN can already be found in the early texts produced by Luther Blissett. What intrigued us most was the way the Zapatistas avoided framing their struggle in any of the hopelessly worn-out twentieth-century modes of thought, and refused old dichotomies such as Reformist vs Revolutionary, Vanguard vs Masses, Violence vs Non-violence, etc. The Zapatistas evidently belonged to the Left, but they refused any linear, traditional left-to-right scale thought, and in a way that had nothing to do with how some European fascists argue that they are 'neither left nor right'. The Zapatista language moved away from stereotypical 'third-worldism': through creative reappropriation they turned old myths, folk tales, legends and prophecies into a vision that encompassed a new transnationalism (Huey P. Newton might have called it 'Intercommunalism'). The 'community' that the Zapatistas talked about was an open one; it went beyond the boundaries of the ethnic groups they spoke for. 'We are all Indians of the world', they stated. They came from the most miserable corner of the known world, and yet they soon got in touch with rebels all around the globe.

The Zapatistas' strategy of communication was based on the refusal of traditional, camera-craving leaders. In the early days of the Levantamiento, Marcos stated: 'I don't exist, I'm just the frame of the window.' He explained that 'Marcos' was just an alias, and he was a just a 'sub-commander', a spokesperson for the Indios. He asserted that everybody could be Marcos, which was the meaning of the balaclavas that the Zapatistas wore: the revolution has no face because it has all faces. 'If you want to see the face under the balaclava, grab a mirror and look at yourself,' Marcos said.

That's where Luther Blissett originated. Commentators have speculated on the alleged 'situationist origins' of the project (a dead-end street if there ever was one), whereas the truth was under everyone's nose. The example set by the Zapatistas helped the LBP refine its purpose: to snatch the use of myths out of the hands of reactionaries.

The Luther Blissett Project was roughly a Five Year Plan, and it lasted from 1994 to 1999. Hundreds of people all over Italy, and in some other countries, adopted the name and contributed to media hoaxes, radio programmes, fanzines, videos, street theatre, performance art, radical politics and theoretical writings. At least fifty agitators remained active in Bologna from beginning to end. In 1995 some of them started to play with the idea of writing a historical novel. That novel was to become *Q*.

As charged as we were with fresh Zapatista suggestions, we almost immediately thought of recounting a peasant insurrection, nay, the mother of all modern insurrections, peasant or not.

We already knew about Müntzer. One member of the Project had briefly belonged to a marxist group where reading Friedrich Engels's *The Peasant War in Germany* was little short of mandatory. And it may sound strange for a Catholic country, but Italy has an interesting tradition of studies on Müntzer and the radical wings of the Reformation. Müntzer's sermons were first published in Italian in 1970. During the Seventies, a highly politicized decade in Italy, the figure of Müntzer was intensely studied and discussed. In such a crucial year as 1989, scholars from different parts of Europe (including the soon-to-collapse East Germany) came to Ferrara – about twenty miles from Bologna – and took part in a conference called 'Thomas Müntzer and the Revolution of the Common Man'.

But why tell that story once again? Why write a historical novel on such an anachronistic subject? What meaning could Thomas Müntzer and the Peasants' War have in the 'roaring 1990s'? 'Communism' had been defeated, 'democracy' had won, belief in free trade was undisputed, to the extent that the French called it *la pensée unique*, 'the only thought'.[2] Market-centric 'neoliberal' ideology was triumphant. Did we really want to write a novel on some long-forgotten proto-communist bums?

Yes, we did. In times of counterrevolutionary hybris, at the peak of 'the greediest decade in history' (as Joseph Stiglitz called it), we thought such a book was more necessary than ever.

Very soon, we came across a work by German playwright Dieter Forte, a 1970 drama entitled *Luther, Müntzer and the Bookkeepers of the Reformation*. It was an explicit allegory of the 1968 movement in West Germany. That text had a powerful effect on us. It kickstarted the writing process.

To tell the truth, the Peasants' War and Müntzer's preaching were just the beginning of the story we would tell. Q covers more than thirty years of European history, from 1517, when Luther nailed his ninety-five theses on the door of the Wittenberg cathedral, to the Peace of Augsburg in 1555. Those tumultuous years have provided historians and storytellers with a host of models and first attempts prefiguring practically every revolutionary strategy and tactic that was to follow. If we listen attentively to what the sixteenth century has to say, we encounter anarchists, proto-hippies, utopian socialists, hardcore Leninists, mystical Maoists, mad Stalinists, the Red Brigades, the Angry Brigade, the Weathermen, Emmett Grogan, punk rock, Pol Pot and Comrade Gonzalo (of Peru's Shining Path guerrilla movement). Also, we find all kinds of culture jammers, body artists, pamphleteers and fanzine publishers. The main character of our novel Q, the nameless hero, gets involved in each and every subversive project he bumps into, from the Peasants' War to the Anabaptist takeover of the city of Münster, from Jan van Batenburg's *Zwaardgeesten* terrorist sect to the Loyalist community in Antwerp, from book-smuggling in Switzerland and Northern Italy to his final escape from Europe towards the Ottoman Empire. The third part of the novel echoes such Luther Blissett practices as the dissemination of false news and the creation of a virtual character (Titian the Anabaptist) with the purpose of bewildering the powers that be.

Nevertheless, there's little doubt that Müntzer is one of the key figures in the novel. He's the character that most impresses himself on the memory of the readers.

What we wanted to do was write a fierce and passionate book, a book that was conscious of itself as a cultural artifact (nay, a cultural weapon), but at the same time didn't raise the usual shield of postmodern detachment. A novel announcing the return of radical/popular narrative fiction. The world needed adventure novels written by folks who were serious about their writing, folks willing to soil their hands without ducking responsibility, or ducking *accountability*.

In March 1999, the publication of Q was our final contribution to the Luther Blissett Project, which ended that year. When the novel was published in the UK, British novelist Stewart Home described it as an example of 'proletarian postmodernism', with the stress put on the adjective rather than the noun. Such temporary classifications always signal that a change is taking place. Later on, the literary tendency that blossomed in the wake of Q was called 'New Italian Epic'.[3]

2. MÜNTZER MOJO RISING, OR, THE CASTLE
UNDER SIEGE (1999–2001)

They say that they are new, they christen themselves by acronyms: G8, IMF, WB, WTO, NAFTA, FTAA... They cannot fool us, they are the same as those who have come before them: the écorcheurs that plundered our villages, the oligarchs that reconquered Florence, the court of Emperor Sigismund that beguiled Ian Hus, the diet of Tuebingen that obeyed Ulrich and refused to admit Poor Konrad, the princes that sent the lansquenets to Frankenhausen, the impious that roasted Dozsa, the landlords that tormented the Diggers, the autocrats that defeated Pugachev, the government whom Byron cursed, the old world that stopped our assaults and destroyed all stairways to heaven.

Nowadays they have a new empire, they impose new servitudes on the whole globe, they still play the lords and masters of the land and the sea.

Once again, we the multitudes rise up against them.

– *From The Multitudes Of Europe*
Rising Up Against The Empire, 2001

The publication of *Q* was followed by an extended book tour all over Italy (and Ticino, the Italian-speaking canton of Switzerland). We met hundreds of readers in all kinds of venues (squats, libraries, bookshops, festivals, etc.), answered their questions and discussed the reception of the book within literary scenes. During that tour we announced that, after the end of the LBP, we would start a new project. It would be more tight-knit and focused on storytelling, with no deadlines. 'Wu Ming' was just around the corner.

We were still travelling when the Battle of Seattle broke out.

It was November 30, 1999. That evening we met with readers of *Q* at the municipal library in Lodi, a small town in Lombardy. Instead of talking about the book, we raved about what had just happened at the WTO summit. We felt it was the beginning of something big.

And it grew to be very big indeed. Very soon, the new movement erupted into a worldwide challenge to the global institutions regulating 'free markets' from the top down: the International Monetary Fund, the World Bank, the World Trade Organization and other bloodsuckers.

The year 2000 was a time of intense organization, protest and disruption of important summits. The most relevant demonstrations took place in Prague at the end of September, when thousands of demonstrators ridiculed an IMF/WB joint meeting. We were there as well.

At a certain point, the movement decided that the showdown – the litmus test of its strength – would be in the third week of July 2001 in Genoa, Northern Italy, where a G8 summit was scheduled. It would be the first G8 summit since the election of George W. Bush as president of the US, and the first with right-wing clown Silvio Burlesquoni as Italian premier and grinning host of the event.

In April 2001, people from all parts of North America gathered in Quebec City to protest against the FTAA treaty. The marches were colourful and radical; the protest was imaginative and multifarious. Many different strands of radicalism twisted together to form ropes, not only metaphorical but also *literal* ropes, with grappling hooks attached to pull down the 'Wall of Shame' (the fence surrounding the summit area). We were there, too, and we thought it was a useful experience, as well as a good omen for Genoa.

In the meantime, curious things were happening in Italy and elsewhere. At demonstrations you saw people resembling Bibendum, the Michelin Man: they wore helmets, white boiler suits and, under the suits, any kind of bodily protection they could find: shoulder pads, shin-guards, life-jackets, cushions, even sheets of packing foam. You'd see hundreds of those funny figures holding big plastic shields or mobile barricades made of tyres, marching towards the coppers in a phalanx-like formation. They had no offensive weapons, only inventive ways of preventing the truncheons from smashing their bones. It was called 'padded civil disobedience', or 'civil disobedience *all'italiana*'. There was something distinctly 'Blissett-like' in that puzzling practice, and we soon started cooperating with those people, mostly orphans of the orphans of the old *Autonomia* movement.

The white overalls are not a uniform, and the images they conjure up should never be of a militaristic kind. That would be a big political mistake.

The white overalls do not fix an identity, nor they have to do with belonging to a group or a troop. The white overalls are a tool. One should never say: 'I belong to the white overalls,' but: 'I'm wearing white overalls.'

White overalls are awkward and clumsy, many times they have been compared to Michelin Men. They can't help laughing at each other, and when the police charge they can't run, they're easy targets, it's like hitting a cow in a corridor [...] The performances in white overalls are aimed at tickling the throats of jolly people [...] Their slogans are ironical in a warm way: the words 'Peace & Love' are associated with pictures of riots, and they chant 'We're coming! / Hey, bastards, we're coming!' on the chorus of *Guantanamera* as they march with both hands raised, perfectly aware that they're going to be clubbed, and none of them will fight back.

The narratives that the white overalls produce about themselves are self-sarcastic, e.g. *The Fable of the White Monkey* [...] The white overalls are consciously ludicrous, that's been their advantage so far. When they cease to be ludicrous, we'll have to find another tool.

– Wu Ming 1, 'An Open Letter to
Limes Magazine' (unpublished), June 2001

It wasn't the only strange phenomenon we detected in those days, for the ghost of Thomas Müntzer (none other!) was reappearing in unexpected places.

There was some kind of short circuit between Q and the movement. Thanks to word of mouth and the Internet, the novel had become an international bestseller. We began to see Müntzer's sentence, '*Omnia sunt communia*' ('All things are to be shared') on banners and placards. We began to see quotations from Q used by activists as email signatures. In forums dedicated to the movement, people would adopt such aliases as 'Magister Thomas' or 'Gert-from-the-Well'. It was only the beginning of a strange, controversial, troublesome relationship between our literary efforts and the ongoing struggle. In the months leading up to the Genoa showdown, the names 'Wu Ming' and 'Wu Ming Foundation' came to be associated more with 'agit-prop' activities than our literary output. It was mainly our fault, as we plunged into the struggle so deeply that it became difficult to avoid confusion of roles. For example, even if it had no byline, everybody knew we were responsible for the epic appeal known as *From The Multitudes of Europe...*, which in the spring and early summer of 2001 was constantly forwarded, printed on leaflets and in journals, broadcast on the radio, scribbled on walls and so on.

Quite obviously, Müntzer was one of the ancestors claimed by the 'narrating we' of the edict: 'We are the army of peasants and miners that followed Thomas Müntzer. [...] The Lansquenets exterminated us in Thuringia, Müntzer was torn to pieces by the headsmen, and yet nobody could deny it: all that belonged to the earth, to the earth would return.'

The text is a declaration of war. A political and historical war, but also a trans-historical and trans-political one. The powerful of the Earth gathered in Genoa for the G8 summit, as well as their educated and overpayed consultants and collaborators, shall not have to face the 'people of Seattle', the students, the thugs of the social centres plus some poor sods and freaks strumming guitars or breaking windows. Or rather, all those people will be there, but together with them, behind them, *inside* them an immense Army of the Dead will be marching. And the text calls on those fallen ones, it makes a list of those troops covered with the dust of centuries and dispersed by the wind of history, with the epic punctilious-ness of Homer's 'Catalogue of Ships'.

– Historian Franco Cardini,
L'Espresso magazine, June 22, 2001

We also wrote or co-wrote plenty of other texts (including *The Fable of the White Monkey*), as well as scripts for street perform-ances and media stunts.

Looking back, we think that Müntzer's ghost appeared at the centre of the mobilization because a general metaphor was taking shape in its midst: empire was described more and more often as a castle besieged by a manifold army of peasants. That metaphor recurs in several texts and speeches. Sometimes it's explicit, very often it's only implied, but it's there. Its emer-gence was influenced by several factors:

1. The summits were invariably held in heavily militarized areas (sometimes called 'red zones'), which conjured up images of a regime under siege by protesters. Demonstrations took the form of 'blockades': the more the power wanted to keep the people out and away, the more the people forced the powerful to meet in ridiculously over-fortified garrisons. Metaphorically speaking, they closed themselves into castles.

2. The movement had a firmly held (and loudly stated) eco-logical stance, and the struggle against Genetically Modified Organisms was diffuse, especially in Europe. In France, José Bové's Confédération Paysanne (Peasant Confederation) was very active in destroying GMO crops and trashing McDonald's restaurants.

3. The popularity of the Zapatistas – a rural, peasant movement – was reaching ever new heights among activists in Europe and North America.

4. The movement's World Forum repeatedly took place in Porto Alegre, Brazil, a country where a radical peasant movement – the Movimento Sem Terra – was active and widespread.

Although it was inspiring and effective, the metaphor was a misrepresentation. There was no real siege going on, as you can't besiege a power that's everywhere and whose main manifestation is a constant flow of electrons from stock exchange to stock exchange.

That misrepresentation would prove fatal in Genoa. We were mistaking the power's formal ceremonies for the power itself. We were making the same mistake Müntzer and the German peasants had made. We had chosen one battleground for our supposed field-day. We were all heading to Frankenhausen.

3. FRANKENSTEIN IN FRANKENHAUSEN (2001–2009)

'How long have you been on the run?'

[…] 'I told you, ever since priests and prophets claimed a hold of my life. I fought with Müntzer and the peasants against the princes. Anabaptist in the madness that was Münster. Purveyor of divine justice with Jan Batenburg. Companion of Eloi Pruystinck among the free spirits of Antwerp. A different faith each time, always the same enemies, one defeat.'

– Luther Blissett, *Q*

Thomas Müntzer spoke to us, but we couldn't understand his words. It wasn't a blessing, but a warning.

It is impossible to disclaim the responsibility the Wu Ming collective had, at least in Italy. We were among the most zealous in urging people to go to Genoa, and helped to steer the movement into the ambush. After the bloodbath, it took quite a while – and a lot of reflection on our part – to understand our own specific errors in the context of the general errors made by the movement.

We had underestimated the enemy, and overestimated ourselves. Clearly, something had gone wrong with the practice of 'mythopoesis' or 'myth-making from the bottom up', which was – and still is – at the core of our philosophy.

By 'myth' we never meant a false story, the most banal and superficial use of the term. We always used the word to signify a narrative with a great symbolic value, a narrative whose meaning is understood and shared within a community (e.g., a social movement) whose members tell it to one another. We've always been interested in stories that create bonds between human beings. Communities continuously share such stories and, as they share them, they (hopefully) keep them alive and inspiring. Ongoing narration makes them evolve, because what happens in the present changes the way we recollect the past. As a result, those tales are modified according to the context and acquire new symbolic/metaphorical meanings. Myths provide us with examples to follow or reject, give us a sense of continuity or discontinuity with the past, and allow us to imagine a future. It's the way our mind works, and we couldn't live without them. Our brains are 'wired' to process reality through narratives, metaphors and allegories.

At a certain point, a metaphor may suffer sclerosis and become less and less useful, until it gets void of all meaning, a disgusting cliché, an obstacle to the growth of inspiring stories. When this happens, people have to veer off, looking for other words and images.

Revolutionary and progressive movements have always found their own metaphors and myths. Most of the time these myths outlive their usefulness and become alienating. Rigor mortis sets in, language becomes wooden, metaphors end up enslaving the people instead of setting them free. The subsequent generation often reacts by negating the past and developing iconoclastic attitudes. The vanguard of each generation of radicals describe the myths they inherit as nothing more than false stories. Some demand that the radical discourse be 'de-mythologized', be it in the name of Reason, 'political correctness', nihilism or even plain stupidity (as in the argument that myths are intrinsically fascist).

No one can erase mythological thought from human communication, because it's embedded in the circuitry of our brains. Cognitive scientists and linguists such as George Lakoff are proving that beyond doubt. We think through metaphors and narratives.

Every iconoclasm eventually generates a new iconophilia, against which new iconoclasts will rage. The cycle will be endless if we don't understand the way these narratives work. The trouble with myths is not their intrinsic falsehood, truth ... or 'truthiness'. The trouble with myths is that they sclerotize easily if we take them for granted. The flow of tales must be kept fresh and lively; we have to tell stories by ever-changing means, angles and points of view, give our tales constant exercise so they don't harden and darken and clog our brains.

This, of course, is an extremely hard task, for several reasons.

First of all, it's too easy to underestimate the dangers of working with myths. One always runs the risk of playing Dr Frankenstein or, even worse, Henry Ford. We can't create a myth at will, as though on an assembly line, or evoke it artificially in some closed laboratory. To be more exact: we could, but it would have unpleasant consequences.

Expanding some observations by Károly Kerényi, Italian mythologist Furio Jesi drew a sharp distinction between a 'genuine' approach to myths and a forced evocation of myths for a specific (usually political) purpose. Think of Mussolini describing the 1937 invasion of Abyssinia as 'the reappearance of the Empire on the fateful hills of Rome'. Kerényi and Jesi called the latter strategy 'technification of myths'.

Technified myth is always addressed to those Kerényi called 'the sleeping ones', i.e., people whose critical attitude is dormant, because the powerful images conveyed by the technifiers have overwhelmed their consciousness and invaded their subconscious. For example, we may 'fall asleep' during the incredibly beautiful first half-hour of Leni Riefenstahl's *Olympia* (1938).

On the contrary, a 'genuine' approach to myths requires staying awake and being willing to listen. We have to ask questions and listen to what myths have to say, we have to study myths, go looking for them in their territories, with humbleness and respect, without trying to capture them and forcibly bring them to our world and our present. It is a pilgrimage, not a safari.

Technified myth is always 'false consciousness', even when we think we're using it to a good purpose. In an essay entitled 'Literature and Myth', Jesi asked himself: 'Is it possible to induce the people to behave in a certain way – thanks to the power exerted by suitable evocations of myths – and then induce them to criticize the mythical motives of their behaviour?' He answered himself: 'It seems practically impossible.'

In the heyday of the alter-globalization movement (from autumn 1999 to summer 2001), we tried to operate in the space between the adverb 'practically' and the adjective 'impossible'. We tried to use the adverb to break open the adjective. We deemed Jesi's answer too pessimistic. We thought that 'opening the laboratory' and showing the people how we processed 'mythologemes' – i.e. the basic conceptual units, the metaphoric 'kernels' of mythological narratives – was enough to provide the people with the tools of criticism. 'Correct distance' from a myth was our chimera: not too close, lest we fall into a stupor, but not so far that we no longer feel its power. It was a difficult balance to maintain, and in fact we didn't maintain it.

We were unable to maintain the balance because the problem is also: who is the artificer of mythopoesis, the evocator, the obstetrician? It should be up to a whole movement or community or social class to handle myths and keep them on the move. No particular group can appoint itself to that office. At the end of the day, we ended up being 'officials' assigned to manipulate metaphors and evoke myths. Our role became a quasi-specialized one. An agit-prop cell. A combo of spin doctors. Sure, *From the Multitudes of Europe…* could make your nerves sing; it made you feel like going to Genoa right away, but that was not enough. We never looked for ways to 'criticize the mythical motives of our behaviour'. 'Practically' never cracked 'impossible'.

At present, there is no alternative to carrying on with the work. We have to continue exploring myths in a way that's not instrumental. We have to understand the nature of myths without wishing to reduce their complexity and without testing their aerodynamic properties in the wind tunnel of politics.

What happened in Genoa was not a 'military' defeat: it was a cultural catastrophe. The tragedy was not only being defeated in the street (which it was). The tragedy was being defeated as a cultural wave. After Genoa, the movement was no longer able to communicate in effective ways, and the media sucked all our blood.

July 20, 2001. That Friday afternoon, on that long street called Via Tolemaide, nobody wore white overalls. A few days before, we all decided to extend the practice of 'padded civil disobedience' as widely as possible. Even such an open symbol as the overalls would stand in the way of that purpose. The *tute bianche* were increasingly being described as an organization, a separate – albeit large – group, and the 'Bibendum' tactic ran the risk of being associated exclusively with those activists. That's why we all decided not to wear the overalls in Genoa. Thus, it was only as a reference to a shared practice that the marchers pouring out of the Carlini Stadium described themselves as 'the disobedients'.

Then the *carabinieri* murdered Carlo Giuliani, and all demonstrations disbanded because of overwhelming police brutality. Thousands of people had to fight their way back to the stadium, like the Warriors gang returning to Coney Island.

That night we felt like pigeon-shooting targets. Everybody was scared, yet we had to respond and take the streets again. At that point, our only hope was that as many people as possible would come to Genoa to show their solidarity. The next day, 300,000 people turned up to save our sorry arses. They were not hardcore militants; the hardcore militants were already in town. They were ordinary people with progressive feelings, outraged by the carnage they'd seen on TV. We will be grateful to that multitude for as long as we live. That Saturday afternoon, we committed to never betray those people. Salvation lay in being open-minded, honest and comprehensible. Salvation lay in keeping away from sectarianism.

It was then that we instinctively started to work on a new mythologem, one that would imply the criticism of the previous ones: Genoa as Frankenhausen.

A guy eavesdropping our conversation asked: – Who the fuck is this Frank Enhausen you keep talking about?

Less than two months after Genoa came the terror attacks of September 11. The situation in the country and in the world got much tougher, and the metaphor of the 'siege' was turned upside down. In 2003 the Italian movement was already in a deep crisis. Not even mass mobilization against the war on Iraq could infuse new energy into its body. At last, it regressed to a marginal presence, a presence occupying the semantic space of traditional far-leftist discourse. The usual boring role played by boring rules. A bunch of 'professional revolutionaries' took over what was left, made all kinds of mistakes and proved to be immensely inadequate for the task. Fossilized sub-Leninist tactics and strategies resurfaced. A lot of time and energy was dissipated in intra-group identity wars. Meetings became pathetic cockfights. The majority of sensitive, 'unregimented' activists (especially women) got bored and quit. We were among those who quit.

In the meanwhile, a self-professed vanguard of the ex–*tute bianche* had embarked on new projects that we regarded as grotesque, projects whose description is clearly beyond the scope of this text. The collaboration between us and that network had lasted little more than a year. So passes a glory of this world.

Since then, we have devoted our time and effort to tightening the bolts of our literary project, writing new novels and essays, and expanding our presence in culture and the cultural industry.

We didn't give up the struggle, far from it, but never again will we play Frankenstein with technified myths.

We keep going, and Don Durito's army of animals keep going, and no defeat is definitive, and hearts are still beating.

July 2008–October 2009

Suggested Further Reading

EDITIONS OF MÜNTZER'S WRITINGS

The Collected Works of Thomas Müntzer, translated and edited by Peter Matheson, Edinburgh: T&T Clark, 1988.

Revelation and Revolution: Basic Writings of Thomas Müntzer, translated and edited by Michael G. Baylor, Bethlehem, PA: Lehigh University Press, 1993.

BIOGRAPHICAL, HISTORICAL AND THEORETICAL STUDIES

Alain Badiou and François Balmès, *De l'idéologie*, Paris: Maspero, 1976.

Peter Blickle, *The Revolution of 1525*, Baltimore: Johns Hopkins University Press, 1985.

Peter Blickle, *From the Communal Reformation to the Revolution of the Common Man*, Leiden: Brill, 1998.

Ernst Bloch, *Thomas Müntzer als Theologe der Revolution*, Frankfurt: Suhrkamp Verlag, 1985.

Norman Cohn, *The Pursuit of the Millennium: Revolutionary Millenarians and Mystical Anarchists of the Middle Ages*, London: Pimlico, 1993.

G. R. Elton, *Reformation Europe 1517-1559*, London: Fontana, 1963.

Frederick Engels, *The Peasant War in Germany*, Moscow: Progress Publishers, 1977.

Lucien Febvre, *Martin Luther: A Destiny*, London: J. M. Dent, 1930.

Abraham Friesen, *Thomas Müntzer, a Destroyer of the Godless: The Making of a Sixteenth-Century Revolutionary*, Berkeley: University of California Press, 1992.

Hans-Jürgen Goertz, *Thomas Müntzer: Apocalyptic, Mystic and Revolutionary*, Edinburgh: T&T Clark, 1993.

Karl Kautsky, *Communism in Central Europe in the Time of the Reformation*, Whitefish: Kessinger, 2008.

Tommaso La Rocca, *Es ist Zeit. Apocalisse e storia. Studio su Thomas Müntzer*, Bologna: Cappelli, 1988.

Tommaso La Rocca (ed.), *Thomas Müntzer e la rivoluzione dell'uomo comune*, Torino: Claudiana, 1990.

Gordon Rupp, *Patterns of Reformation*, London: Epworth, 1969.

Tom Scott, *Theology and Revolution in the German Reformation*, Basingstoke: Macmillan, 1989.

Jakob Taubes, *Occidental Eschatology*, Stanford: Stanford University Press, 2009.

George Hunston Williams, *The Radical Reformation*, Kirksville: Truman State University Press, 2001.

Chronology of Thomas Müntzer's Life[1]

c. 1488	Birth in Stolberg, Harz, probably from a craftsman father and a peasant mother.
1506	Enrols at the arts faculty of the University of Leipzig.
1512	Registered at the University of Frankfurt (Oder), where he receives a master of arts and bachelor of holy scripture.
1513	Vicar at Halle.
1514	Ordained as a priest at Halberstadt.
1516	Priest and confessor at the convent at Frose near Aschersleben. Becomes involved with the anti-clerical religious circle around the trader Hans Pelt in Brunswick. Travels intensively in central-northern Germany and becomes acquainted with the social conditions of peasants and town-dwellers.
1518	Goes to Wittenberg, where he meets Luther and strikes up friendships with Melanchthon and Agricola. Studies scripture, Patristics, the writings of Luther, Karlstadt, Melanchthon, classical rhetoric and Plato.

1519
Involved in the controversy between Franciscans and the followers of Luther in Jüterborg, where he delivers a number of anti-clerical sermons. From May onwards, he is confessor at the convent at Benditz, where, hoping to come to grips with the decay of Christianity, he reads Josephus, Eusebius and Augustine. He also acquaints himself with German mysticism (Henry Suso, Johannes Tauler and the *Theologia Deutsch*).

1520
Called by the council, he becomes a preacher in Zwickau, a thriving trade and mining town in Thuringia. Moves from the main church of St Mary's to the main church of St Catherine's, frequented by the poorer sectors of Zwickau society. Comes under the influence of the cloth-worker Nicholas Storch and the Anabaptist 'Zwickau prophets', with whom he joins in the struggle against the rich notables and their pastor, Silvius Egranus.

1521
Stoked by the unrest of the cloth-workers, who were faced with a growing gap between prices and wages, and by Müntzer's anti-clerical preaching in favour of the lower classes, the situation comes to a head. In April, Müntzer is dismissed, triggering an armed revolt among the poorer citizens. Flees to Bohemia, home to a number of anti-clerical movements and of considerable social turmoil. In Prague, he attempts to found a 'new apostolic church' of the elect. The authorities eventually bar him from the town's pulpits. In November, he writes *The Prague Protest*.

1522
A period of restless movement. Müntzer preaches in different towns (Erfurt, Nordhausen, Stolberg, Weimar, Glauchau near Halle).

1523   Appointed pastor in Allstedt. Reforms the
method of worship: the Latin Mass is abolished
and German liturgy introduced. Publishes a
number of liturgical texts, as well as *Protestation
or Proposition* and *Counterfeit Faith*, signalling his
definitive break with Luther. Tensions mount
with Count Ernst von Mansfeld, who forbids
his subjects from attending Müntzer's German
liturgy. Founds the 'League of the Elect'.
Müntzer marries Ottilie von Gersen, a runaway
nun.

1524   Following a sermon by Müntzer, the chapel of
the Virgin Mary in Mallerbach is burnt down.
Müntzer is blamed for the iconoclastic act.
Müntzer asks to preach before Duke John and
his son John Frederick, in order to counter
attacks against him by the Wittenbergers. The
Sermon to the Princes calls on the princes to
adopt Müntzer's radical standpoint or have
sovereignty wrested from them by the common
people. Tensions escalate in Allstedt and nearby
Sangerhausen. On July 24, Müntzer preaches
the need for a covenant to defend the common
people against the authorities. The 'League' is
renewed and Müntzer himself signs up, alongside
various townspeople and Mansfeld miners, in
an 'emergency act of self-defence' against the
'godless'. The men, women and girls of Allstedt
arm themselves. On August 1, he is summoned
to defend himself at Weimar, his printing press
is shut down and the dissolution of the League is
decreed. Luther publishes his *Letter to the Princes
of Saxony Concerning the Seditious Spirit*. Müntzer
flees Allstedt. He arrives in Mühlhausen, where
the common citizens had been in conflict with
the council and clergy for some time. He forms
an alliance with the former monk Heinrich
Pfeiffer, and in September they briefly take
control of the city council. Müntzer participates

in drawing up the Eleven Articles of the town's new constitution, which are aimed at establishing a direct democracy for the common people. The experiment collapses, and Müntzer flees to Nuremberg. Responding to the attacks of Luther and the princes, he publishes the *Special Exposure of False Faith* and the *Highly Provoked Defence*. He is forced to flee Nuremberg. Müntzer spends the winter between Swabia, Switzerland and the Black Forest, agitating among the peasants.

1525   Returns to Mühlhausen in February. The 'Eternal Council' is established, and Müntzer promotes a democratic republican constitution, as well as the military defence of the town. Though the new council represents a partial compromise with the town's property owners, Müntzer regards Mühlhausen as the fulcrum of the rebellion against the princes. He works to establish alliances between peasants, miners and town-dwellers. Luther publishes his libel *Against the Thieving and Murderous Peasant Hordes*. Müntzer and Pfeiffer lead raids on cloisters and castles. On May 12, Müntzer arrives at Frankenhausen, where about eight thousand rebellious peasants have already gathered. On May 15, after the assembled peasants reject the demand to hand over Müntzer, the princes' armies strike. They crush the peasants, who suffer over six thousand dead over against six dead from the princely armies. Müntzer flees but is soon captured and handed over to Count Ernst von Mansfeld. He is imprisoned and tortured at the castle of Heldrungen. He writes a *Confession*, a letter to the people of Mühlhausen and a (disputed) *Recantation*. On May 27, Thomas Müntzer is beheaded, along with Pfeiffer. Their heads and bodies are impaled and put on display.

Note on Texts

The texts that follow reproduce the Michael G. Baylor translation, first published by Associated University Presses in 1993 as *Revelation and Revolution: The Basic Writings of Thomas Müntzer*. In the preface to that edition, Baylor writes, 'As a result of his study of the Vulgate, Müntzer was sensitive to the problem of how literal or free to make translations of centuries-old sources in a foreign language. His interest in the "living spirit" of a text rather than its "dead letter" suggests his point of view. In the preface to his *German Evangelical Mass* he acknowledged that he translated "more according to the sense than according to the words." I too have taken a number of liberties with the format and the literal meaning of Müntzer's writings; the reader should be warned of these concessions to the modern ear. In many cases I have added paragraph divisions where Müntzer moves forward without benefit of a longer pause. Even more frequently I have broken up Müntzer's long, complex sentences. Other forms of punctuation – dashes, semi-colons, quotation marks, etc. – have been freely introduced. Müntzer made use of parentheses to set off certain remarks, and, where these are found, they are his. The material that I have interpolated into the texts has been placed in brackets . . . There are a few other ways in which the literal form of the originals have been changed. Müntzer commonly used familiar second-person verb and pronoun forms, but I have rejected the English equivalents as archaic. His repetitive and sometimes confusing use of connective words (*da, deshalb, aber,* etc.) has occasionally been altered or omitted. The names of people and places and the few titles of the literary works he mentioned have been modernized.'

I

The Prague Protest[1]

A PROTEST ABOUT THE CONDITION OF THE BOHEMIANS

I, Thomas Müntzer, born in Stolberg and residing in Prague, the city of the precious and holy fighter Jan Hus,[2] think that the loud and moving trumpets [that once sounded in this city] were filled with the new praise of the holy spirit. With my whole heart, I will testify about my faith and lamentingly complain about present conditions to the whole church of the elect and to the whole world, wherever this document may be received. Christ and all of the elect who have known me from my youth on confirm such a project.

I pledge on my highest honour that I have applied my most concentrated and highest diligence in order that I might have or obtain a higher knowledge than other people of the foundations on which the holy and invincible Christian faith is based. The truth makes me so bold as to say that no pitch-smeared parson and surely no pseudospiritual monk can say anything about the foundation of the faith in even its smallest point. In addition many people have complained with me that they, too, burdened by the unbearable and evident deception of the clergy, were never consoled, and that they have had to direct their desires and works carefully in the faith themselves and to elevate themselves spiritually. The clergy have never been able to discover, nor will they ever, the beneficial tribulations and useful abyss that the providential spirit meets as it empties itself.[3] The spirit of the fear of God has never possessed the clergy, but the elect firmly cling to this spirit as their only goal. The elect are submerged and drowned in an outpouring of this spirit (which the world cannot tolerate). In brief, each person must receive the holy spirit in a sevenfold way, otherwise he neither hears nor understands the living God.

Freely and boldly I declare that I have never heard a single donkey-cunt doctor of theology, in the smallest of his divisions and points, even whisper, to say nothing of speaking loudly, about the order (established in God and all his creatures). The most prominent among the Christians (I mean the hell-based parsons) have never had even a whiff of the whole or undivided perfection, which is a uniform measure superior to all parts, 1 Corinthians 13[:10], Luke 6[:40], Ephesians 4[:3], Acts 2[:27], 15[:18?], and 17[:24–26]. Again and again, I hear nothing from the doctors of theology but the mere words of Scripture, which they have knavishly stolen from the Bible like malicious thieves and cruel murderers. They will be damned for this theft by God himself, who spoke thusly through Jeremiah 23[:18], 'Behold, I have said to the prophets: I never once spoke to those who steal my words, each from his neighbour, for they deceive my people, and they usurp my words and make them putrid in their stinking lips and whoring throats. For they deny that my spirit speaks to people.' So they display their monasticism with flattering, high mockery. And they say that the holy spirit gives them an invincible witness that they are children of God, Romans 8[:16], Psalm 192.

It is certainly not surprising that these damned people, the clergy, in their impudence are opposed to my teachings. For Jeremiah (in the aforementioned chapter 23 [Jer. 23:18]) says of their person, 'Who has stood in the counsel of the Lord?

Who has perceived and heard the speech of God? Who has marked it, or who can say that he has heard God speaking?' At the present time, God will pour forth his invincible wrath over such arrogant people, hardened like blocks of oak, callous to all good, Titus 1[:7], in that they deny the basic salvation of faith. For, otherwise, they would repudiate their lives and defend the elect like an iron wall from the harm of the blasphemers, as Ezekiel says (in chapter 3, etc.). But, as they are, nothing else comes out of their hearts, brains, and snouts than derision about such revelations. Who among all people can still say that these parsons are true servants of God, bearing witness to the divine word? And that they are fearless preachers of divine grace? They have been smeared by the Nimrodian papacy[4] with the oil of the sinner, Psalm 141[:5], which flows from the head down to the feet and befouls and poisons the whole Christian church. That is to say, the parsons come from the devil, who has corrupted the foundation of their heart, as it is written in Psalm 5[:10], for they are entirely without the possession of the holy spirit. Therefore, they have been ordained by the consecration of the devil, their rightful father, who with them cannot hear the true living word of God – John [8:38–44], Isaiah 24[:18], and Hosea 4[:6?]. Zechariah 11[:17] also says that such people are scarecrows in green bean fields.

And in sum, this much can be said: the parsons are damned people, John 3[:18], who have already been long condemned. And indeed they are not the least, but the most highly placed damned rogues, who have been everywhere in the world from the very beginning, set as a plague on poor people, who as a result are truly coarse. These poor people receive absolutely no justice from either God or men, as Paul adequately showed in Galatians [4:22ff.], where he describes two kinds of people.

Therefore, as long as heaven and earth stand, these villainous and treacherous parsons are of no use to the church in even the slightest matter. For they deny the voice of the bridegroom,[5] which is a truly certain sign that they are a pack of devils. How could they then be God's servants, bearers of his word, which they shamelessly deny with their whore's brazenness? For all true parsons must have revelations, so that they are certain of their cause, 1 Corinthians 14[:30]. But the parsons, with their stubborn hearts, say that this is impossible. Because they are convinced of this – after they presume to have devoured the whole of Scripture – they shall be struck down with the words of St Paul, 2 Corinthians 3[:3], as with thunder and lightning, for there Paul makes the distinction between the elect and the damned.

The gospel and the whole of Scripture are closed to some people – Isaiah 29[:11] and 22[:22] on the key of David, Revelation 3[:7] on the locked book. Ezekiel unlocked past events.[6] Christ says in Luke 11[:52] that the parsons will steal the key to this book that is locked. They lock up Scripture and say that God must not speak to people in his own person. But where the seed falls on good ground [Mt. 13:5] – that is, in hearts that are full of the fear of God – this is then the paper and parchment on which God does not write with ink, but rather writes the true holy Scripture with his living finger, about which the external Bible truly testifies.[7] And there is no more certain testimony, as the Bible verifies, than the living speech of God, when the father speaks to the son in the hearts of people. All of the elected people can read this Scripture, for they increase their talent. But the damned will surely let God's living voice pass. Their heart is harder than any flint, and it repels the chisel of the master [God] for eternity. Therefore our dear Lord calls them stone, on which the seed falls and fails to bring forth fruit [Mt. 13:5], although they accept the dead word with joy, great joy, and praise.

Upon my soul, only scholars and priests and monks accept the truth from books with hearty flattery and pomp. But when God wants to write in their heart, there is no people under the sun who are a greater enemy of the living word of God than they. They also suffer no tribulation of faith in the spirit of the fear of God, so they are on their way into the fiery lake, where the false prophets will be tormented with the Antichrist for ever and ever, amen. Moreover, they do not want to be disturbed by the spirit of the fear of God. So they mock the tribulation of faith for eternity. They are precisely the people about whom Jeremiah 8[:8–9] speaks,[8] for they have no experience of holy Scripture that they have sensed and that they can apply in their exposition. They have no other manner of writing than that of hypocrites, who throw away the truthful word and all the same need it. So they will never hear it in an eternity of eternities. For God speaks only in the suffering of creatures, a suffering that the hearts of the unbelievers do not have because they become more and more hardened. Unbelievers can and will not empty themselves. They have a slippery foundation and loathe their owner [God]. Therefore, in a time of tribulation, they collapse. They retreat from the word that became flesh. In no way does the unbeliever want to become conformed to Christ through suffering; rather he seeks conformity only with honey-sweet thoughts.

Therefore, it is these damned parsons who take away the true key [to divine truth] and say that such a way [as direct revelations] is fantastic and fool-headed, and that it is most impossible. These are the ones already condemned, with skin and hair, to eternal damnation. Why should I not damn them as well? John 3[:18] Since they are not sprinkled with the spirit of the fear of God on the third day, how can they be cleansed on the seventh day? Numbers 19[:19] So they have already been cast into the abyss of the pit [hell].

But I do not doubt the [common] people.[9] Oh, you righteous, poor, pitiful little band! How thirsty you still are for the word of God! For now are the days when none, or only a few, know what they should hold or which side they should join. They would gladly do what is best, and yet they do not know what this is. For they do not know how to conform to or comply with the testimony that the holy spirit speaks in their hearts. They are so greatly disturbed by the spirit of the fear of God that in them the prophecy of Jeremiah [4:4] has indeed become true, 'The children have prayed for bread and there was no one there to break it for them.' Oh, oh, no one broke it for them! There have been many money-hungry rogues who have thrown to the poor, poor, poor little people the inexperienced papal text of the Bible, as one usually throws bread to dogs. But they have not broken it with the knowledge of the holy spirit. That is, they have not opened their reason, so that they might recognize the holy spirit in themselves. For the parsons, even if they were all gathered together in one pile, do not have the power to make a single individual sufficiently sure that he has been chosen for eternal life. What more can I say?

Parsons are lords, who only devour, swill, and steal, day and night seeking to contrive how they can feed themselves and get many fiefs, Ezekiel 34[:2, 8, 10]. They are not like Christ, our beloved Lord, who compares himself to a hen that makes her chicks warm. Nor do they give milk to the disconsolate, forsaken people from the fountain of the inexhaustible admonitions of God. For they have not tested their faith. They are like a stork that gobbles up frogs in the fields and ponds, and then afterwards spits them out, just as raw, to its young in the nest. So, too, are the profit-seeking and interest-boosting parsons who gobble whole the dead words of Scripture and then spit out the letter and their inexperienced faith (which is not worth a louse) to the righteous, poor, poor people. The result of what they do is that no one is certain of his soul's salvation. For these servants of Beelzebub bring to market only a fragment of holy Scripture. Indeed, no one knows if he is worthy of God's love or hate. This poison comes out of the abyss, for each and every whoremongering priest has the devil as his most deceitful and villainous prince, as the Revelation of John [Rev. 13:4–8] proclaims.

The parsons scatter the sheep of God so widely through this evil that no one looks to the church any more. For no one there separates good people from the impudent band that is unknown [to God]. There is also no knowledge of the diseased and the healthy – that is, no one pays attention to the fact that the church is rotten to its floor and foundations with damned people. For the sheep do not know that they should hear the living voice of God. That is, they should all have revelations, Joel 2[:28–29] and David in Psalm 87[:7]. The office of the true shepherd is simply that the sheep should all be led to revelations and revived by the living voice of God, for a master should teach the knowledge of God, Matthew 23[:10, 26]. This has not happened for a long time, and, as a result, the elect and the damned are just the same in many respects, and the elect have been almost swallowed up by the damned. Therefore, nearly the whole world also thinks that it is not necessary that Christ himself must preach his own gospel to the elect.

I affirm and swear by the living God: he who has not heard the righteous, living word of God out of the mouth of God, [and can discern] what is Bible and what is Babel, is nothing but a dead thing. However, the word of God penetrates the heart, brain, skin, hair, bones, limbs, marrow, juice, force, and power. It is able to stride in a different way from that about which our foolish, scrotum-like doctors of theology prattle. Otherwise, one can neither be saved nor found. The elect must clash with the damned, and the power of the damned must yield before that of the elect. Otherwise you cannot hear what God is. Whoever has once received the holy spirit as he should, can no longer be damned, Isaiah 55[:3] and 60[:15, 21], John 6 [Rev. 6:44–5]. Oh ho, woe, woe to those preachers who proclaim the way of Baal! For they have uttered the words in their snouts, but their hearts are more than a thousand times a thousand miles away from the word.

Thus, people live without true shepherds. The experience of faith is never preached to them. The Jewish, heretical parsons[10] may well say that such a strong thing is not necessary for salvation. They say that one can indeed flee the wrath of God with good works, with precious virtues. However, the people do not learn from all this what God is in experience, what true faith is, what strong virtue is, and what good works are after conversion to God. Therefore it would not be surprising if God were to destroy us all, the elect with the damned, in a much more severe deluge than that of former times, and crumble us to dust and rubble in body and life. And it would also be no surprise if he were to damn all the people who have suffered these cursed seductions. For is our faith indeed not oriented more to the face of Lucifer and Satan than to that of God? And the devil is coarser than wood and stone.

In my view it is not without reason that all other peoples call our faith monkey business. For it is evident and cannot be denied that unbelievers have demanded a serious accounting from us. And we have returned an answer from a chicken coop – with immense pride we have spattered great books full, saying, 'We have written this and that in our laws; for if Christ said this, Paul has written that; the prophets have foretold this and that; holy mother church (a madam in a whorehouse) has proclaimed this and that.' Indeed, the Nero-like, 'holy,' most wooden pope and chamber pot at the brothel of Rome has commanded this and that great thing, defending them with the ban of excommunication. And in the opinion of the little straw doctors of theology, for the sake of the conscience this ban is not to be despised.

My good reader, let the words [of the Bible] simply be different or arranged differently. Then our theologians could not defend the Christian faith with their inexperienced Bible, no matter how great the twaddle they talk. Oh, alas, alas, woe, woe, woe to the hell-fiery and Asmodaeical parsons[11] who publicly seduce the people.

Yet no one wants to see or hear it when such reasons for our faith, and similar ones, are presented to unbelievers. Do you not think that non-Christians, too, have a brain in their heads? They may indeed think to themselves, What kind of assurance of faith is this which comes from books? Perhaps [the authors of Scripture] have lied in what they have written? How can one know whether it is true? Without a doubt Turks and Jews would gladly hear our invincible basis for believing, and many of the elect would also like the same thing. But the devil's parsons wrinkle up their noses and damn them forthwith. And yet the parsons cannot judge correctly, since they deny that a person can have revelations. They speak with the mere words of Scripture, 'He who believes and is baptized will be saved' [Mark 16:16]. Such a firmly grounded account, and no other, they give to our opponents. It cannot be otherwise, nor do I perceive it differently, than that the parsons who thus seek to expound the faith so badly to our enemies are completely mad and foolishly inane. One should call such rascals to account, and those who offer such a lame excuse should be shoved into the abyss of hell. Is not this [defence of the faith] much more insane than insanity itself? Who can complain about it and bemoan it enough? Do we lack blood in our body and life that affairs proceed in such a mad and stupid way?

Does one not feel at least a small spark that virtually seeks to expand into tinder? Indeed, one feels it and I feel it too. I have very bitterly pitied the fact that the Christian church has become so badly crushed that God could only do it more damage if he wanted to annihilate it altogether. But God would not want to do this except for the diarrheamakers [the clergy], for they have taught the people to pray to Baal. They are so highly 'worthy' that one may say in the midst of them what Daniel says [Dan. 9:5, 10], that they have not practised the judgments of God.

I have read here and there in the histories of the ancient fathers of the church. And there I find that, after the death of the pupils of the apostles, the untarnished, virgin church soon became a whore at the hands of seducing parsons. For parsons have always wanted to have a ruling position in the church. Hegesippus and Eusebius and others testify to all this. [The downfall of the church came about] because the people neglected to exercise their right to elect their priests. And it has not been possible to hold a true council since the onset of such negligence. Be this as it may, it is still the work of the devil, for matters are only treated in councils and synods as they would be in a child's game. Things dealt with are the ringing of bells, chalices, hoods, lamps, and [ecclesiastical titles like] procurators and sextons. But no one has once – no, not once! – opened his snout concerning the true, living word of God. Nor has any thought been given to the proper liturgy.

Such errors had to occur so that the works of all people, the elect and the damned, would be fully manifest. In our time God wants to separate the wheat from the chaff [Mt. 13:26], so that one can grasp, as though it were bright midday, who it is that has seduced the church for such a long time. All the villainy, even in the highest places, must come to light. Oh ho, how ripe are the rotten apples! Oh ho, how mushy the elect have become! The time of the harvest is at hand! Thus God himself has appointed me for his harvest. I have made my sickle sharp, for my thoughts are zealous for the truth and my lips, skin, hands, hair, soul, body, and my life all damn the unbelievers.

In order that I may do this properly, I have come into your country, my most beloved Bohemians. I desire from you only that which your diligence should demand – you should study the living word of God out of God's own mouth. Through this you will see, hear, and grasp how the whole world has been seduced by deaf parsons. Help me, for the sake of Christ's blood, to fight against such high enemies of the faith. In the spirit of Elias, I want to ruin them in your eyes. For the new apostolic church will arise first in your land, and afterward, everywhere.

I want to be prepared, if in church people question me in the pulpit, to do enough to satisfy each and every one. If I cannot demonstrate such a skilful mastery of the truth, then may I be a child of both temporal and eternal death. I have no greater pledge. Whoever despises such warnings as these is already, now, in the hands of the Turks. After this raging conflagration, the true Antichrist will personally reign, the radical opposite of Christ. And shortly after this, Christ will give to his elect the kingdom of this world for all eternity.

Given to Prague on the day of St Catherine [25 November] in the year of our Lord 1521.

Thomas Müntzer will not pray to a dumb God, but rather to one who speaks.

2

Sermon to the Princes (or An Exposition of the Second Chapter of Daniel)

An Exposition of the Second Chapter of Daniel the Prophet, preached at the castle of Allstedt before the active and dear dukes and rulers of Saxony by Thomas Müntzer, servant of the word of God.
Allstedt, 1524.[1]

FIRST

The text of the abovementioned chapter of the prophecy of Daniel the prophet was set forth and translated [from the Vulgate] in its clear literal sense, and then the whole sermon, with the correct context, was set down as follows:

It is to be understood that poor, miserable, disintegrating Christendom can neither be counselled nor assisted unless diligent, indefatigable servants of God promote the Bible daily by reciting, reading, and preaching. But if this is done, either the head of many a pampered cleric must suffer a continuous rain of hard blows, or he will have to give up his profession. How can this be avoided when Christendom is being so terribly devastated by ravaging wolves? – as it is written about the vineyard of God in Isaiah 5[:1ff.] and Psalm 80[:9–14]. And St Paul teaches in Ephesians 5[:19] how one should train oneself in the recitation of divine praises.

At the time of the beloved prophets Isaiah, Jeremiah, Ezekiel, and the others, the whole community of God's elect had fallen so totally and completely into idolatrous ways that even God himself could not help the people. Instead, he had to let them be led away into bondage and suffer long among the heathen until they again acknowledged his holy name, as it is written in Isaiah 29[:17–24], Jeremiah 15[:11–14], Ezekiel 36[:20ff.], and Psalm 89[:31–38]. And just as it was then, it is no less true that, in the time of our forefathers and in our own time, poor Christendom has become much more petrified and has only an inexpressibly slight resemblance to its divine name, Luke 21[:5], 2 Timothy 3[:5]. And the devil and his servants finely adorn themselves with this semblance, 2 Corinthians 11[:13ff.]. Indeed, they adorn themselves with it so attractively that the true friends of God are seduced by it, and, even with the most practised zeal, they are scarcely able to recognize their error, as Matthew 24[:24] clearly shows.

All this has been brought about by the contrived holiness and hypocritical forgiveness of sins practised by the godless enemies of God, since they assert that the Christian church cannot err. But to the contrary, in order to guard against error the church should be constantly built on the word of God and thus kept free from error. Yes, the true church should also acknowledge the sin of its own ignorance, Leviticus 4[:13f.], Hosea 4[:6], Malachi 2[:1–7], and Isaiah 1[:10–17]. For it is surely true that Christ, the son of God, and his apostles – indeed, even his holy prophets before him – began a true, pure Christendom, for they cast the seed of pure wheat in the field. That is, they planted the true word of God in the hearts of the elect, as is written in

Matthew 12 [see, rather, Mt. 13:3–23], Mark 4[:3–20], Luke 8[:5–15], and Ezekiel 36[:29]. But the lazy, negligent ministers of this same church have not wanted to maintain this work and bring it to fruition through diligent care. Rather, they have pursued their own selfish interests and not those of Jesus Christ, Philippians 2[:21].

Therefore, the clergy permitted the damage of the godless – that is, the tares[2] – to spread in its strength, Psalm 80[:9–14]. For the cornerstone [Christ] referred to here in the second chapter of Daniel [Dan. 2:34–44] was still small. Isaiah 28[:16] also speaks of it. To be sure, it has not yet come to fill the whole world, but it will soon fill it and make it full, ever so full. Thus, in the beginning of the new Christendom, the established cornerstone was soon rejected by the masons – that is, by the rulers, Psalm 118[:22f.] and Luke 20[:17f.]. Therefore, I say that the church, begun in this way, has become dilapidated everywhere, down to the present time of the divided world, Luke 21[:10], and here Daniel 2[:35] and Ezra 4[:1–5]. For Hegesippus says, and Eusebius says in the twenty-second chapter of book IV on the Christian church, that the Christian community did not remain a virgin any longer than up to the time of the death of the disciples of the apostles. And soon afterward it became an adulteress, as had already been prophesied beforehand by the beloved apostles, 2 Peter 2[:14]. And in the Acts of the Apostles, St Paul said to the shepherds of the sheep of God with clear, ringing words, Acts 20[:28–31], 'Take heed, therefore, unto yourselves and unto the whole flock, which the holy spirit has placed you to watch over, that you should feed the community of God, which he has purchased through his blood. For I know that after my departure ravaging wolves which will not spare my flocks will come among you. Also, from among yourselves men will arise who will promulgate perverted teachings to attract the younger disciples to themselves. Therefore, watch out!' The same thing stands written in the letter of the holy apostle Jude

[Jude 4:19], and Revelation 16[:13f.] points to it as well. There-fore, our Lord, Christ, warned us to guard against false prophets, Matthew 7[:15].

Now, it is as clear as day – and may God hear our com-plaint – that nothing is as badly and as little respected today as the spirit of Christ. And yet no one may be saved unless this same holy spirit has previously assured him of his salvation, as it is written in Romans 8[:6], Luke 12[:8], John 6[:63] and 17[:2–31]. But how do we poor little worms expect to reach this while we regard the worthiness of the godless with such respect that unfortunately Christ, the gentle son of God, appears before the great titles and lineages of this world like a scarecrow or a painted puppet? And yet he is the true stone that will be cast down from the high mountain [Dan. 2:45] into the sea, Psalm 46[:3], because of the pompous opulence of this world. He is the stone who was torn from the great mountain without human hand, the stone who is called Jesus Christ, 1 Corinthians 10[:4]. He was born just at the time when the evil of slavery prevailed, Luke 1[:52] and 2[:1], at the time of Octavian, when the whole world was in motion and was being counted.[3] Then Octavian, one who was spiritually without any power, a miser-able scumbag, wanted to have power over the whole world, which was of no use to him except for his own luxury and arro-gance. Indeed, he let himself think that he alone was great. Oh, how very small then was the cornerstone, Jesus Christ, in the eyes of men! He was banished to a stable, like an outcast among men, Psalm 22[:7]. Accordingly, the scribes rejected him, Psalm 118[:22], Matthew 21[:42–46], Mark 12[:10–12], Luke 20[:17–19], as they still do today.

Indeed, since the death of the beloved disciples of the apos-tles, these scribes have even reenacted the Passion with him. They have turned the spirit of Christ into a laughingstock, and they continue to do so, as is written in Psalm 69[:11ff.]. They have most blatantly stolen him, like thieves and murderers, John

10[:1]. They have robbed Christ's sheep of their true voice and made the true crucified Christ into a completely fantastic idol. How has this come about? My answer is that they have rejected the pure knowledge of God and, in its place, they have set up a pretty, fine, golden image of God. Before it, the poor peasants smack their lips, as Hosea has clearly said in chapter 4[:6–13], and as Jeremiah said in Lamentations 4[:5], 'Those who formerly ate fine spiced food have now received instead dirt and filth.' Oh, how unfortunate is the pitiful abomination of which Christ himself spoke, Matthew 24[:15], foreseeing that he would be so wretchedly mocked by the devilish offering of Mass, the superstitious preaching, the ceremonies, and the manner of living. And even so, the whole time, there is nothing there but a mere wooden idol. Indeed, there is only a superstitious, wooden parson and a coarse, loutish, and rude people, who cannot grasp the slightest assertion about God. Is this not a pity, a sin, and a scandal? I believe most assuredly that the beasts of the belly, Philippians 3[:19], and the swine written about in Matthew 7[:6] and 2 Peter 2[:22] have trampled underfoot the precious stone, Jesus Christ, as completely and totally as they have been able. He has become a doormat for the whole world. For this reason all the unbelieving peoples, Turks, heathens, and Jews, have mocked us in the vilest way and taken us for fools – as one should regard senseless people who do not want to hear the spirit of their faith mentioned. Thus, the suffering of Christ is nothing but the baiting at a market festival and the disparaging of rogues, as Psalm 69[:11–12] says, which not even a lowly foot soldier has had to endure.

Therefore, dear brothers, we should come out of this filth and become true pupils of God, taught by God, John 6[:48], Matthew 23[:8–10]. Then we will need God's great powerful strength, which will be granted us from above, in order to punish and annihilate such unspeakable wickedness. This knowledge is the most clear wisdom about God, Proverbs 9[:10], which springs only from a pure, uncontrived fear of God. This same fear alone must arm us with a mighty hand for revenge on the enemies of God and with the highest zeal for God, as stands written in Proverbs 5[:18], John 2[:17], and Psalm 69[:9, 18, 24]. There is certainly no excusing God's enemies with human or rational considerations, for the appearance of the godless is beautiful and deceptive beyond all measure, like the beautiful cornflower among the golden ears of wheat, Ecclesiastes 8[:14]. But the wisdom of God must recognize such deceit.

SECOND

We must examine more closely and correctly the abomination that despises this stone. But so that we correctly recognize the abomination in the godless, we must daily expect God's revelation. Oh, that has become the most precious and rare thing in this corrupt world! For [unless we expect revelations], the sly schemes of the clever ones could overcome us at any moment and keep us still more from the pure knowledge of God, Proverbs 4[:12], Psalm 37[:14–32]. Such a thing must be forestalled by the fear of God.

Only if this same fear is completely and purely anchored in us can holy Christendom easily return again to the spirit of wisdom and the revelation of the divine will. All this is encompassed in Scripture, Psalm 145[:18f.], Psalm 111[:5–10], Proverbs 1[:7]. But the fear of God must be pure, without any admixture of human or 'creaturely' [i.e., materialistic and selfish] fear, Psalm 19[:10], Isaiah 66[:2], Luke 12[:4f.]. Oh, this fear is very necessary for us! For just as one can scarcely serve two masters, Matthew 6[:24], so one can scarcely fear both God and creatures. Nor may God himself have mercy on us (as the mother of Christ our Lord says) unless we fear him alone with our whole heart. Therefore, God says, 'If I am your father, where then is the honour due me? If I am your lord, where then is fear of me?' Malachi 1[:6].

So, you dear princes, it is necessary in these most dangerous days, 1 Timothy 4[:1f.], that we apply the greatest diligence to combat such underhanded evil, as have all our beloved ancestors who are recorded in the Bible from the beginning of the world. For the time is dangerous and the days are evil, 2 Timothy 3[:1–8], Ephesians 5[:15f.]. Why? Only because the noble power of God has been so miserably disgraced and dishonoured that the poor, coarse people are seduced by the great blubbering of unsaved scribes. The prophet Micah in chapter 3[:11] says about them that this is the nature of nearly all the scribes with very few exceptions: they teach and say that God no longer reveals his divine mysteries to his beloved friends through valid visions, his audible word, or other ways. Thus the scribes remain bogged down in their inexperienced ways, Ecclesiastes 34[:10]. And they have coined a gibe against people who go about with revelations from God, as the godless did to Jeremiah in chapter 20[:7f.], 'Listen, has God spoken to you recently? Or have you directed your questions to the mouth of God lately and taken counsel with him? Do you have the spirit of Christ?' The scribes do this with great scorn and mockery.

Was it not a great thing that took place in the time of Jeremiah? Jeremiah warned [Jer. 20:4–5] the poor, blind people about the punishment of captivity in Babylon, just as pious Lot warned his sons-in-law, Genesis 19[:14]. But this warning appeared to the people to be most foolish. The blind people said to the beloved prophet, 'Yes, yes, God should indeed warn the people in such a paternal way.' But what happened then to the mocking crowd during the Babylonian captivity? Nothing, except that they were brought to shame by this heathen king, Nebuchadnezzar. Behold the text [of Dan. 2:47] here! Nebuchadnezzar had received the proclamation of God, and, nevertheless, he was a powerful tyrant and a punishing rod for the people of the elect who had sinned against God. But, because of the blindness and stubbornness of the people of God, the most exalted goodness of the world had to be proclaimed in such a way, as St Paul in Romans 11[:22] and Ezekiel 23[:22–35] say.

Thus, for your instruction here, I, too, say that the omnipotent God not only revealed to the heathen king those things that were many years in the future – to the unspeakable disgrace of the proud among the people of God who did not want to believe any prophet. The untested people of our time are exactly the same – they are not conscious of the punishment of God, even when they see it right before their eyes. What shall almighty God then do with us? He must withdraw his goodness from us.

Now we come to the biblical text of Daniel 2, 'The king Nebuchadnezzar had a dream which vanished from him,' etc. What should we say about this? It is an unspeakable, indeed an abnormal and hateful thing to speak about people's dreams.[4] The reason for this is that the whole world, from the beginning down to the present time, has been deceived by dreamers and interpreters of dreams, as is written in Deuteronomy 13[:2ff.] and Ecclesiastes 34[:7]. So it is shown, in this chapter of Daniel, that the king did not want to believe the clever fortune-tellers and dream interpreters. For he said, 'Tell me my dream and only then the interpretation. Otherwise you will tell me nothing but mere deception and lies.' What happened then? They were not able to do this and could not tell him the dream. And they said, 'Oh, beloved king, no man on earth is able to tell you your dream. Only the gods can do this, who have nothing on earth in common with human beings.' Yes, to be sure, according to their understanding they spoke correctly and in a reasonable way. But they had no faith in God. Rather, they were godless hypocrites and flatterers, who said then what the rulers gladly wanted to hear, just as the scribes do now in our time, those who gladly want to eat tasty tidbits at court. But opposing

them is that which is written in Jeremiah 5[:13–31] and 8[:8f.].
And how much more is written there! The text of Daniel says
here [Dan. 2:28] that there must have been people then who
had fellowship with God in heaven. Oh, for the clever ones that
is a bitter herb to swallow. But St Paul wants to have it so, too,
Philippians 3[:20]. And, nevertheless, such learned ones immediately want to explicate the secrets of God. Oh, the world has
now had more than enough of these rogues, who publicly presume to do such things.

And God says in Isaiah 58[:2] about these scribes, 'They want
to know my ways just as the people do who have fulfilled my
righteousness.' Such scribes are like fortune-tellers, since they
openly deny any revelation from God and hence assault the holy
spirit in his handiwork. They want to instruct all the world.
And what does not conform to their inexperienced understanding they immediately ascribe to the devil. And yet they are not
even assured of their own salvation, although this assurance is
necessary, Romans 8[:14ff.]. They can babble beautifully about
faith and brew up a drunken faith for the poor, confused consciousness of the people. All this comes from their indecisive
judgment and from the abomination. They have derived this
view from the contemptible deception of the most damnable,
poisonous monks' dreams, through which the devil has effected
all his plans. Indeed, this teaching has also irretrievably deceived
many pious people among the elect. For, without any instruction from the spirit, they have given themselves over without
hesitation to these visions and dreams of their crazy faith. And
so from the revelations of the devil, monastic rules and sheer
idolatry have been written down. St Paul vigorously warned
against this in his letter to the Colossians 2[:8]. But the damnable monkish dreamers have not known how they can become
conscious of the power of God. Therefore, their perverted
minds are hardened. And they are now shown before the whole
world, more clearly from day to day, to be nothing except sin

and shame – like do-nothing scoundrels. They are still blind in their stupidity. Nothing else has misled them, and nothing else even to the present day seduces them further than this superstition. This is so because, without any experience of the advent of the holy spirit – the master of the fear of God – they despise knowledge of God and fail to separate good from evil which is concealed under the appearance of good. God cries out about this through Isaiah 5[:20], 'Woe unto you who call good evil and evil good!' Therefore, it is not the manner of pious people to reject the good along with the evil. For St Paul says to the Thessalonians 5 [1 Th. 3:20f.], 'You should not despise prophesying. Test all things but hold fast to what is good,' etc.

THIRD

You should also know that God is so completely and totally well disposed toward his elect that if he could warn them in the smallest matters, Deuteronomy 1[:42] and 36 [see, rather, Dt. 32:6, 29], Matthew 23[:37], he would most certainly do it – if they could receive this same warning despite the magnitude of their unbelief. For here this text of Daniel agrees with what St Paul wrote to the Corinthians in chapter 2 [1 Cor. 2:9f.] – and is taken from holy Isaiah 64[:3] – saying, 'What no eye has seen, what no ear has heard, and what has not come into any human heart, this God has prepared for those who love him. But God has revealed this to us through his spirit. For the spirit searches all things, yes also the depth of the godhead,' etc.

In brief, it is an earnest conviction of mine that we must know and not only believe in an empty way whether what has been given us is from God or the devil or from nature. If we want to be able to make our natural understanding of these same matters obedient to faith, 2 Corinthians 10[:5], then reason must be led to the ultimate limit of its capacity for judgment, as is shown in Romans 1[:16ff.] and Baruch 3 [see, rather, Jer. 45:3]. But natural reason can in good conscience make no certain judgment without God's revelation. For people will clearly find that they cannot attain heaven with their heads. Rather, they must first become in an interior way complete and utter fools [to the world],[5] Isaiah 29[:13f.] and 33[:18], Obadiah 1[:8], 1 Corinthians 1[:18ff.]. Oh, that is a very alien message to the clever, carnal, and sensual world. For when it is received, there immediately follow pains like those of a woman giving birth, Psalm 48[:7], John 16[:21]. For Daniel and every pious person with him finds that it is just as impossible for him to acquire by natural reason a knowledge of God as it is for the rest of the common people. This is what the wise prophet means, Ecclesiastes 3[:11], for he says, 'He who wants to discover the majesty of God will be crushed by his magnificence.' For the more natural reason strives for God, the further the working of the holy spirit distances itself, as Psalm 139[:6] clearly shows. Indeed, if one understood the pretensions of natural reason, without a doubt one would not seek much help from stolen Scriptures, as the scribes do with a scrap or two of text, Isaiah 28[:10], Jeremiah 8[:8]. Rather, he would soon feel how the working of the divine word springs from his heart, John 4[:14]. Indeed, he would not need to carry stagnant water to the well, Jeremiah 2[:13], as our scribes now do. They confuse nature with grace, without drawing any distinction. They obstruct the way of the word, Psalm 119[:110], which arises from the abyss of the soul. As Moses says, Deuteronomy 30[:14], 'The word is not far from you. Behold, it is in your heart,' etc.

Now, perhaps you ask how it is that the word comes into the heart? The answer is: when the striving for truth is strong, it comes down to us from God above – which I will let stand for now and say more about at another time. And this striving for truth, whether what is called God's word is really God's or not, begins when one is a child of six or seven years of age, as is symbolized in Numbers 19[:19f.]. Therefore St Paul cites Moses [Dt. 30:14] and Isaiah [65:1] in his letter to the Romans 10[:8]. And he speaks there of the inner word to be heard in the abyss of the soul through the revelation of God. And the person who has not become conscious of and receptive to this inner word, through the living testimony of God, Romans 8[:9], does not know how to say anything essential about God, even though he may have devoured a hundred thousand Bibles.

From this, anyone can easily measure how far the world really is from the Christian faith. Still, no one wants to see or hear it. Now, if a person should become conscious of the word and receptive to it, God must remove all his carnal desires. And if the impulse from God comes into his heart, so that he wants to kill all the desires of the flesh, it is necessary that the person then give way to God, so that he may receive his action. For a bestial person does not perceive what God speaks in the soul, 1 Corinthians 2[:14]. Rather, the holy spirit must refer him to the serious contemplation of the plain, pure meaning of the law, Psalm 19[:8]. Otherwise, he remains blind in his heart, and he fantasizes for himself a wooden Christ, and he misleads himself.

Therefore, look at how repugnant it became for beloved Daniel [Dan. 2:18] to interpret the vision to the king and how diligently he thus beseeched God and prayed to him! To have revelations from God, therefore, one must cut himself off from all diversions and have a serious desire for truth, 2 Corinthians 6[:17]. And through practising such a [method of discovering] truth, he must learn to distinguish the undeceived vision from the false one. Thus, beloved Daniel says, in chapter ten, 'A person must have the right method of understanding visions in order to know that they are not all to be rejected,' etc.

FOURTH

You should know that an elected person who wants to know which visions or dreams are from God and which are from nature or the devil must be severed in his mind and heart, and also in his natural understanding, from all temporal reliance on the flesh. And it must happen to him as it happened to beloved Joseph in Egypt, Genesis 39 [rather, Gen. 40:5–20], and also to Daniel here in this second chapter. For a sensual man, Luke 7[:25], will accept nothing but the pleasures of the world, which are thistles and thorns, as the Lord says, Mark 4[:7, 18], and he will suppress the whole manifestation of the word that God addresses in the soul. For this reason, if God has already spoken his holy word in the soul, the person cannot hear it if he is inexperienced. For he does not look within or see into himself and into the abyss of his soul, Psalm 49[:21]. Such a man does not want to crucify his life, with his lusts and appetites, as Paul the holy apostle teaches [see Gal. 5:24]. Thus, the plowed field of the word of God remains full of thistles and thorns and full of much underbrush. These must all be removed for the work of God to take place, in order that the person is not found to be negligent or lazy, Proverbs 24[:30f.]. And, after these hindrances have been removed, one sees the fruitfulness of the field and finally the good crop. Only then does the person become aware that he is the dwelling place of God and the holy spirit for the duration of his days. Indeed, he sees that he has been truly created for one purpose only, that he should seek the testimony of God in his own life, Psalm 93[:4] and 119[:95–125]. He will perceive these testimonies at first only in part, through visual means, and then perfectly in the abyss of his heart, 1 Corinthians 13[:10ff.].

In the second place, he must take note that such visual images and symbols in dreams or visions approximate in every respect those which are testified to in the holy Bible, so that the devil does not intrude next to them and spoil the balm of the holy spirit with his diabolical sweetness, as the wise man says of the flies that die from this sweetness, Ecclesiastes 10[:1].

In the third place, the elected person must pay attention to the manner in which the visions occur. They must not pour forth swiftly through human machinations. Rather, they should simply flow out according to God's irrevocable will. And the elected person must take heed most carefully that not a particle of that which he has seen is lost, so that its effect can be fully reproduced. But when the devil wants to do something, he is betrayed by his lazy posturing, and his lies finally peek out, for he is a liar, John 8[:44].

In this chapter of Daniel the same point is clearly demonstrated by King Nebuchadnezzar and, afterward, is shown in fact in the third chapter. For the king quickly forgot the warning of God. Without a doubt, this was caused by his carnal desires, which he directed towards pleasures and creaturely things. It must always happen in this way when a person wants constantly to cultivate his own pleasures and yet also have something of God's action and not be in any tribulation. In this condition the power of the word of God cannot overshadow him, Luke 8[:12–14]. God the almighty shows true dreams and visions to his beloved friends most often in their deepest tribulation, as he did to pious Abraham, Genesis 15[:1–6] and 17[:1ff.]. God appeared to him as he shuddered in terrible fear. Similarly, as beloved Jacob fled with great tribulation from his brother, Esau, a vision came to him in which he saw a ladder extended up to heaven, with the angels of God climbing up and down on it, Genesis 28[:12]. Afterward, when he came home again, he had a tremendous fear of his brother Esau. Then the Lord appeared to him in a vision in which God crushed his hip and struggled with him, Genesis 32[:25f.]. And similarly, pious Joseph was also hated by his brothers, and, in this tribulation, he had two visions of danger, Genesis 37[:5–11]. And afterward, in his heartfelt tribulation while imprisoned in Egypt, Joseph was so greatly enlightened by God that he could interpret all visions and dreams, Genesis 39[:21], 40[:12–19] and 41[:25ff.].

More than all these examples, that other Joseph, in Matthew 1[:20–23] and 2[:13, 19f., 22], should be held up before the untempted, pleasure-seeking swine who think they are such clever little ones. This Joseph had four dreams when he was terrified by his tribulation, and, through the dreams, he was reassured. So, also, in their sleep the wise men were instructed by an angel not to return to Herod [Mt. 2:12]. Similarly, the beloved apostles were diligently attentive to visions, as is clearly described in their history, the book of Acts. Indeed, it is a truly apostolic, patriarchal, and prophetic spirit that awaits visions and attains them in painful tribulation.

Therefore it is no wonder that Brother Fattened-swine and Brother Soft-life [Luther] rejects visions, Job 28[:12]. But if a person has not perceived the clear word of God in his soul, then he must have visions. So it was that St Peter, in the Acts of the Apostles, did not understand the Mosaic Law of Leviticus, chapter eleven, and had doubts about the cleanliness of food and about whether to have anything to do with heathens, Acts 10[:10f.]. And then, in the fulness of his mind, God gave him a vision. In it he saw a linen cloth with four corners stretching down from heaven to earth, and it was filled with four-footed animals. And he heard a voice saying, 'Slaughter and eat.' The devout Cornelius had a similar experience when he too did not know what he should do, Acts 10[:3–6]. And when Paul came down to Troas, a vision appeared to him in the night. It was a man from Macedonia, who stood before him and greeted him and said, 'Come down to Macedonia and help us.' After he had seen such a vision, says the text of Acts 16[:8ff.], 'Soon thereafter we tried to travel to Macedonia for we were certain that the Lord had called us there.' And similarly, when Paul was afraid to preach in Corinth, Acts 18[:9f.], the Lord said to him through a vision in the night, 'You should not be afraid,' etc. 'No one shall attempt to do you harm for I have many people in this city,' etc.

And what need is there to bring forth the many other witnesses of Scripture? In such momentous and dangerous matters as those which true preachers, dukes, and princes have to deal with, it would never be possible to guard themselves securely against error on all sides, and to act blamelessly, if they did not rely on revelations from God – as Aaron heard from Moses, Exodus 4[:15] and David from Nathan and Gad, 2 Chronicles 29[:25]. For this reason, the beloved apostles were completely and totally accustomed to visions, as the text of Acts 12[:7ff.] proves. There the angel came to Peter and led him out of Herod's prison. And he thought he was having a vision. He did not know that the angel was accomplishing his release by this means. But if Peter was not accustomed to visions, how could it have occurred to him that this was a vision?

From this, I now conclude that whoever is inexperienced and an enemy of visions because of a carnal consciousness, and either accepts them all without any discrimination or rejects them all because the false dream interpreters of the world have done such harm by being greedy and selfish people, this person will not fare well. Rather, he will be in conflict with the holy spirit, Joel 2[:26f.]. For God clearly speaks, as in this text of Daniel, about the transformation of the world. He will bring about this transformation in the Last Days, so that his name will be rightly praised. He will release the elect from their shame and pour forth his spirit over all flesh. And our sons and daughters shall prophesy and shall have dreams and visions, etc. For, if Christendom is not to become apostolic, Acts 27 [see, rather, Acts 2:16ff.], where Joel is cited, why then should one preach? To what purpose then are visions in the Bible?

It is true – and I know it to be true – that the spirit of God now reveals to many elected pious people that a momentous, invincible, future reformation is very necessary and must be brought about. Each one may protect himself against it as he wishes and yet the prophecy of Daniel remains undiminished, though no one believes it, as Paul also says to the Romans 3[:3]. This text of Daniel is thus as clear as the bright sun, and the work of ending the fifth empire of the world is now in full swing.

The first empire was symbolized by the golden head [of the statue in Nebuchadnezzar's dream]. That was the empire of Babylon. And the second empire was represented by the silver breast and arms, which was the empire of the Medes and Persians. The third empire was the empire of the Greeks, which resounded with its cleverness, indicated by the brass. The fourth empire was the Roman empire, which was won with the iron sword and was an empire of coercion. The fifth empire or monarchy is that which we have before our own eyes [i.e., the Holy Roman Empire] and it is also (like the fourth) of iron and would like to be coercive. But, as we see before our very eyes, the iron is intermixed with filth, vain schemes of flattery that slither and squirm over the face of the whole earth.[6] For he who cannot be a cheat [in our empire] must be an idiot. One sees now how prettily the eels and snakes copulate together in a heap. The priests and all the evil clergy are the snakes, as John the Baptist calls them, Matthew 3[:7], and the temporal lords and rulers are the eels, as is symbolized by the fish in Leviticus 11[:10–12]. For the devil's empire has painted its face with clay.

Oh, you beloved lords, how well the Lord will smash down the old pots of clay [ecclesiastical authorities] with his rod of iron, Psalm 2[:9]. Therefore, you most true and beloved regents, learn your knowledge directly from the mouth of God and do not let yourselves be seduced by your flattering priests and restrained by false patience and indulgence. For the stone [Christ's spirit] torn from the mountain without human touch has become great. The poor laity and the peasants see it much more clearly than you do. Yes, God be praised, the stone has become so great that, already, if other lords or neighbours wanted to persecute you on account of the gospel, they would be overthrown by their own subjects. This I know to be true. Indeed the stone is great! The foolish world has long feared it. The stone fell upon the world when it was still small. What then should we do now, after it has grown so great and powerful? And after it has struck the great statue so powerfully and irresistibly that it has smashed down the old pots of clay?

Therefore, you dear rulers of Saxony, stand boldly on the cornerstone, as St Peter did, Matthew 16[:18], and seek genuine perseverance, granted by the divine will. He will surely temper you on the stone, Psalm 40[:3]. Your path will be the right one. Seek unhesitatingly the righteousness of God at all times and bravely take up the cause of the gospel. For God stands so close to you that you do not believe it. Why do you want to be frightened by the spectre of man? Psalm 118[:6].

Look closely at this text of Daniel! King Nebuchadnezzar wanted to kill the clever ones because they could not interpret the dream for him. This was deserved. For, with their cleverness, they wanted to rule his whole kingdom, and yet they could not even do what they had been engaged for. So also are our clergy today. And I tell you this truly: if you were able to recognize the harm that has befallen Christendom and rightly reflect on it, then you would win for yourselves as much zeal as Jehu the king,[7] 2 Kings 9 and 10, and as much zeal as the whole book of the Apocalypse shows. And I know for sure that you would hold yourselves back from exercising the power of the sword only with great effort. For the pitiable corruption of holy Christendom has become so great that at present no tongue can fully express it.

Therefore, a new Daniel must arise and interpret your revelation for you. And this same new Daniel must go forth, as Moses teaches, Deuteronomy 20[:2], at the head of the troops. He must reconcile the anger of the princes and that of the enraged people. For, if you were truly to experience the shame of Christendom and the deception of the false clergy and incorrigible rogues, then no one could imagine how enraged at them you would become. Without a doubt it would gall you, and you would fervently take it to heart that you had been so kind to them after they had led you to the most shameful opinions with the sweetest words, Proverbs 6[:1ff.], and against all established truth. For they have made fools of you, so that everyone now swears to the saints that princes are heathen people insofar as their office is concerned. Princes, they say, should do nothing but maintain civil unity.

Oh, beloved ones, the great stone will indeed soon fall on and smite this view of your office and smash such rational schemes to the ground. For Christ says, in Matthew 10[:34], 'I have not come to bring peace but the sword.' But what should one do with these false spiritual leaders? Nothing but what is done with evildoers who obstruct the gospel: put them away and cut them off, if you do not want to be servants of the devil but servants of God, as Paul calls you in Romans 13[:4]. You should not doubt that God will smash to bits all your adversaries who undertake to persecute you. For as Isaiah 59[:1] says, 'His hand is not yet hampered.' Therefore God is still able to help you and will do so, just as he stood by King Josiah the elect [2 Kg. 22–23], and the others who defended the name of God. Thus, you rulers are angels when you seek to act justly, as Peter says in 2 Peter 1[:4]. Christ commanded this very earnestly, Luke 19[:27], and said, 'Take my enemies and strangle them for me before my eyes.' Why? Ah, because they have spoiled Christ's government, and, in addition, they seek to defend their villainy under the guise of the Christian faith. And, with their deceitful infamy, they pollute the whole world. Therefore Christ our Lord says, Matthew 18[:6], 'Whosoever does evil to one of these little ones, it is better for him that a millstone be hung about his neck and that he be thrown into the depths of the sea.' He who wishes, turning [in his evasions] here and there, can gloss over this. But these are the words of Christ. Now, if Christ can say this about someone who does evil to one of the little ones, what should be said about those who do evil to a great multitude in their faith? For this is how archvillains act, who do evil to the whole world and make it deviate from the true Christian faith, and who say that no one shall know the mysteries of God. Each person should judge them according to their words and not according to their actions, Matthew 23[:3]. They say that it is not necessary for the Christian faith to be tested like gold in the fire, 1 Peter 1[:7], Psalm 140[:11]. But if this were the case, the Christian faith would be worse than the faith of a dog that hopes to get a scrap of bread while the table is being set. False scribes present such an image of the faith to the poor, blind world. This suits them, for they preach only for the sake of their belly, Philippians 3[:19]. From their hearts they can say nothing else, Matthew 12[:34].

Now, should you want to be true rulers, then you must begin government at the roots, as Christ commanded. Drive his enemies away from the elect, for that is your appointed task. Beloved ones, do not offer us any stale posturing about how the power of God should do it without your application of the sword. Otherwise, may the sword rust away in its scabbard on you. May God grant this!

Let any scribe say whatever he wants to you. Christ's words are sufficient, Matthew 7[:19], John 15[:2–6], 'Every tree that does not bring forth good fruit should be uprooted and cast into the fire.' If you now remove the mask from the world, then you will soon recognize it for what it is with a righteous judgment, John 7[:24]. Judge righteously, as God commands! You have sufficient help for the purpose, Proverbs 6[:16–23], for Christ is your master, Matthew 23[:8]. Therefore do not permit evildoers, who turn us away from God, to live longer, Deuteronomy 13[:6]. For a godless person has no right to life when he hinders the pious. In Exodus 22[:1] God says, 'You shall not permit the evildoer to live.' St Paul also means this, for he says that the sword of rulers is given for the punishment of evildoers and to protect the pious, Romans 13[:1–4]. God is your guardian and he will teach you to struggle against his enemies, Psalm 18[:35]. He will make your hands skilful in fighting and he will also sustain you. But in addition you will have to suffer a great cross and temptation, so that the fear of God is made clear to you. This cannot happen without suffering. But it will cost you no more than the danger that is risked for the sake of God's will and the useless prattle of your opponents. Although pious David was driven from his castle by Absalom, nevertheless, he finally regained it when Absalom was hanged and stabbed [2 Sam. 15:10–18 and 18:9–15]. Therefore, you dear fathers of Saxony, you must risk it for the sake of the gospel. For God will chastise you in a friendly way, as he does his most beloved sons, Deuteronomy 1[:31], when he is burning with his momentous wrath. Then blessed are all those who rely on God. Say freely with the spirit of Christ, 'I will not fear a hundred thousand, even if they have surrounded me.'

At this point I imagine that our scribes will hold up to me the kindness of Christ, which they claim for themselves and use hypocritically. But in contrast to this, they should also look at the wrath of Christ, John 2[:15–17], Psalm 69[:10], with which he tore up the roots of idolatry, as Paul says to the Colossians 3[:5–9]. Because of these scribes, the wrath of God cannot be removed from the community. If, according to our view, he cast down those guilty of lesser offences, then without a doubt he would not have spared idols and images if they had been there. As he commanded through Moses in Deuteronomy 7[:5f.], where he says: 'You are a holy people. You shall not have pity on the idolatrous. Break up their altars. Smash their images and burn them so that I am not angry with you.' Christ has not abrogated these words. Rather, he will help us to fulfil them, Matthew 5[:17]. The visual symbols are all explicated by the prophets, but these are bright clear words that must remain for eternity, Isaiah 40[:8]. God cannot say 'yes' today and 'no' tomorrow. Rather, he is unchangeable in his words, Malachi 3[:6], 1 Samuel 15[:10–22], Numbers 22[:6]. But if it is objected that the apostles did not destroy the idols of the heathen, I reply as follows: St Peter was a timid man, Galatians 2[:11ff.]. He was hypocritical with the heathen. He was also symbolic of all the apostles in this respect, so that Christ said of him in the last chapter of John [Jn. 21:15–19] that he had a very strong fear of death. And it is easy to figure out that Peter acted in this way because he did not want to give the heathen any reason to kill him. But St Paul spoke out most firmly against idolatry, Acts 17[:16–31]. And, if he had been able to carry out his teaching resolutely among the Athenians, without a doubt he would have utterly cast out idolatry, as God commanded through Moses, and as also happened afterward through the martyrs, according to trustworthy histories.

Therefore the deficiency or negligence of the saints gives us no reason to allow the godless to continue in their ways. Since they profess God's name with us, they should choose one of two alternatives – either repudiate the Christian faith entirely or put away their idolatry, Matthew 18[:8f.].

But then our scribes come along and, referring to the text of Daniel, say in their godless, stolen way that the Antichrist will be destroyed without a hand being lifted. This is too much! Anyone who says this is already as fainthearted as the Canaanites were when the elect wanted to enter the promised land, as Joshua [5:1] writes. Joshua nevertheless did not spare them from the sharpness of the sword. Look at Psalm 44[:4] and 1 Chronicles 14[:11]. There you will find the same solution: the elect did not win the promised land with the sword alone, but rather through the power of God. Nevertheless, the sword was the means, just as for us eating and drinking are the means for sustaining life. Thus the sword is also necessary as a means to destroy the godless, Romans 13[:1–4].

But for this use of the sword to occur as it should and in the right manner, our dear fathers who confess Christ with us – that is, the princes – should do it. But if they do not do it, then the sword will be taken away from them, Daniel 7[:27]. For then they confess Christ with words and deny him in their actions, Titus 1[:16]. Thus the princes should offer peace to the enemy, Deuteronomy 2[:26–30]. But if the princes want to be 'spiritual' and not render an account of their knowledge of God, 1 Peter 3[:12–17], they should be got rid of, 1 Corinthians 5[:13]. I, together with pious Daniel, bid them not oppose God's revelation. But, if they do take the contrary course, may they be strangled without any mercy, as Hezekiah [2 Kg. 18:22], Josiah [2 Kg. 23:5], Cyrus [2 Chr. 36:22f.], Daniel [Dan. 6:27], and Elijah, 1 Kings 18[:40] destroyed the priests of Baal. Otherwise, the Christian church will not be able to return to its source. The tares must be pulled out of God's vineyard at the time of harvest. Then the beautiful golden wheat will gain lasting roots and come up right, Matthew 13[:24–30, 39]. The angels who sharpen their sickles for the cutting are the earnest servants of God who fulfil the zeal of divine wisdom, Malachi 3[:1–6].

Nebuchadnezzar perceived this divine wisdom through Daniel [Dan. 2:46f.]. He fell down before him after the mighty truth had overpowered him. He was blown like a straw in the wind, as chapter 3[:26–30] proves. Similarly, there are now innumerable people who accept the gospel with great joy as long as everything is going well for them in a pleasing way, Luke 8[:48]. But when God wants to put such people in the crucible or when he puts them into the fire of a crucial test, 1 Peter 1[:7], oh, then they are angered by the smallest word of the gospel, as Christ proclaimed in Mark 4[:17]. By the same token, without a doubt many untested people will be angered by this booklet, because I say with Christ, Luke 18 [see, rather,

Lk. 19:27], Matthew 18[:6], with Paul, 1 Corinthians 5[:7, 13], and with the instruction of the whole of divine law, that godless rulers, especially the priests and monks, should be killed. They tell us the holy gospel is a heresy, and, at the same time, they want to be the best Christians. Just as their hypocritical, false goodness will turn to rage and become infinitely bitter, it will also defend the godless and say that Christ killed no one, etc. And because the friends of God, most lamentably, are without effective power, the prophecy of Paul is fulfilled, 2 Timothy 3[:1ff.]. In the Last Days the lovers of pleasure will indeed have the appearance of virtue, but they will deny its power. Nothing on earth has a better form and mask than false goodness. Thus, all the corners of the earth are full of absolute hypocrites, among whom none is so bold as to be able to proclaim the real truth.

In order that the truth may really be brought to light, you rulers – God grant that you do not willingly do otherwise – must act according to the conclusion of this chapter of Daniel [Dan. 2:48]. That is, Nebuchadnezzar elevated holy Daniel to office so that the king might carry out good, correct decisions, inspired by the holy spirit, Psalm 58[:11f.]. For the godless have no right to life except that which the elect decide to grant them, as is written in the book of Exodus 23[:29–33]. Rejoice, you true friends of God, that the enemies of the cross have crapped their courage into their pants. They act righteously, even though they never once dreamed of doing so. If we now fear only God, why should we recoil before vacillating, incapable men, Numbers 14[:8f.], Joshua 11[:6]. Only be bold! He to whom is given all power in heaven and on earth [Christ] wants to lead the government, Matthew 28[:18]. To you, most beloved, may God grant eternal protection. Amen.

3

Special Exposure of False Faith

Special Exposure of False Faith, set forth to the unfaithful world through the witness of the Gospel of Luke, in order to remind suffering pitiable Christendom of its false life,[1] Ezekiel 8[:7–10].

'Beloved companions, let us widen the gap, so that the whole world can see and grasp who our mighty ones are, who have so viciously made God into a painted puppet,' Jeremiah 23[:29],

Thomas Müntzer, with a hammer.

Mühlhausen, 1524.

Jeremiah 1[:9f.], 'Behold, I have set my word in your mouth. Today I have set you over the people and over empires, so that you may root out, break up, disperse, and destroy. And so that you may build up and plant.'

Jeremiah 1[:18f.], 'An iron wall has been set up between the kings, princes, and parsons, on the one hand, and the people on the other. They will contend and the victory will be wonderful due to the defeat of the strong, godless tyrants.'

PREFACE TO POOR DISPERSED CHRISTENDOM

The spirit of the strength and fear of God be with you, you piti-able community. After the libellous writings [of Luther] have made you partly fearful – and also most impudent – it is exceed-ingly necessary for me to counter the rising evil with a demon-stration of Christian mastery.[2] At the present time, this mastery cannot be shown except through an exposition of holy Scrip-ture, especially the teachings of the spirit of Christ, and through a comprehensive comparison of all the secrets and judgments of God. For all knowledge contains within itself its diametrical opposite. But where passages of Scripture have not been grasped in their context, no individual passage may be completely and totally understood (no matter how bright and clear it is) without damaging unspeakably the other passages. This error is the basic cause of every evil schism in the Christian community.

For the sake of such an important cause [as scriptural integ-rity], I, an inadequate person, have advanced on the fortress [in which the godless have barricaded themselves] in order to widen the breach in the wall and with the expectation of suf-fering all the evils that the godless despoilers usually impose on the servants of Christendom. They impose these evils after they have elaborately embellished their literalistic faith and denied (this too is palpable) the gracious power of God. And so they want to make God dumb, insane, and fantastic with their false word and false faith. Therefore, the arrogant practice of every abomination among all the communities of the whole world has also made people so proud that from day to day they engage in nonsensical resistance [against true faith]. Thus, a fundamen-tal consideration of the holy Christian faith must turn back the wild upsurge of the rising waves (as described in Psalm 93[:3]). Because no one else wants to grasp the rudder of the ship on account of the difficult effort involved, I cannot release the rudder, since the water of every ruination has penetrated into the souls of the friends of God, Psalm 69[:2]. I must faithfully uncover the poisonous damage which has spread so far. I will gladly do this with all mercy where my critique is accepted. But, where it would redound to the disadvantage of the spirit of Christ, my patience will not conceal the disgrace of anyone whatsoever.

At the beginning of this explanation and exposure of false faith, I always want to let each section follow the other naturally and so allow sufficient space and time [to vindicate myself against] my opponents. But I have only shunned the dangerous corner [of a private disputation] for the reason that the situation demands it. In the same way, Christ himself shunned the viperous scribes, John 7[:32ff.], and would give Annas[3] in a private conversation no other justification for his teaching than that he referred him to his listeners, the common people, John 18[:19–21]. He spoke clearly to Annas: 'Why do you ask me? Ask my listeners.' Our learned ones would gladly like to give the witness of Jesus' spirit a higher education. They will completely fail in this because they are not educated enough to teach so that through their teachings the common man may be brought up to their level. Rather, the learned ones alone want to pass judgment on the faith with their stolen Scripture, although they are totally and completely without faith, either before God or before men. For everyone perceives and realizes that they strive for honours and worldly goods. Therefore, you, the common man, must become learned yourself, so that you will be misled no longer. The same spirit of Christ will help you in this which will mock our learned ones to their destruction. Amen.

EXPLANATION OF THE FIRST CHAPTER OF LUKE

The whole Gospel of Luke gives Christendom a precious testimony in order for it to realize that the holy Christian faith has become such an alien, strange thing that it would not be surprising if a good-hearted person, one who has correctly perceived the blindness of Christendom, were to weep blood. Christ himself spoke about this in the Gospel of Luke 18[:8], saying, 'Do you think that if the son of man were to come, he would find faith on the earth?' Isaiah, too, complains about this in chapter fifteen [see, rather, Is. 65:1ff. or 53:1f.], and Paul in his Letter to the Romans 10[:16,20f.].

Therefore, it is an inexpressible calamity and a completely awful abomination that the unfaithful (as anyone can see with his own eyes) want to preach the Christian faith to the people – a faith that they themselves have not felt and experienced. Nor do they know the feelings of a believer. They think, or deceive themselves into thinking, that faith is as easy to attain as they all blabber about very boastfully.

Therefore, my most beloved brothers, we must earnestly take to heart this first chapter of Luke from start to finish. For, indeed, we will clearly find in it how unbelief is laid bare in all of the elect. Zechariah did not want to believe the word of the angel Gabriel [Lk. 1:11–19], and he reproached Gabriel because what he said was impossible. Mary, the bearer of our saviour, who is therefore praised by the children's children, is also most worthy of consideration [Lk. 1:48]. She wanted to have good reasons and supporting information [for believing what the angel said]. Zechariah and Mary did not attain their faith, as the insane world now believes, in a rosy way. They did not merely go on and say, 'Yes, I will simply believe that God will make everything all right.' With such an easy source of belief, the drunken world concocts a poisonous faith, which is much worse than that of the Turks, heathen, and Jews. But Mary and Zechariah were terrified in the fear of God, until the faith of a mustard seed [Mt. 17:20 and Lk. 17:6] conquered their unbelief.[4] This process is experienced with great trembling and affliction.

Even God cannot increase the faith of anyone and look upon him as saved unless this person has patiently endured the source [of real faith] with the greatest trembling and fear. God himself says this through holy Isaiah 66[:2]: 'Whom should I scrutinize except the lowly and those who are terrified before all my sayings.' Thus Paul says to the Philippians 2[:12], 'You must strive for your salvation with trembling and fears.' Oh ho, the fear of God at the beginning of faith is an unbearable thing to human nature. Moses heard God himself speak. Nevertheless, he did not want to heed his word, since God told him to go into Egypt, Exodus 4[:1ff.]. Moses had to experience the power of God in the abyss of his soul, as he later testified, Deuteronomy 30[:9–14]. Otherwise he would not have gone to Egypt. God promised the patriarch Jacob many goods and infinite security. Nevertheless, he quarrelled with God. He had to fight for a victory over God before he could accept the blessings that faith brings with it, Genesis 32[:25–30].

Thus, every diligent person finds testimony throughout the whole of Scripture, especially in the Book of Judges 6[:13ff.], 7[:7], and 8[:4ff.], of how faith continually contends with unbelief. Gideon had such a firm, strong faith that, with it, he conquered a huge army with only three hundred men. But, before he was willing to accept such a faith, he said to the angel of God, just as one chastises a habitual liar: 'You say the Lord is with you, you almighty man. How can that be when we must suffer so much misfortune?' The person of untrained faith, at the first encounter with God, has no other basis for acting than to be fearful of everything and to be unreachable by the best arguments. For he who easily believes has an easygoing heart. But the fear of God gives the holy spirit an abode, so that God may protect the elect – God, whom the world most foolishly fears, with irreparable harm to its 'wisdom.'

Thus, in this Gospel of Luke, one should especially note the beginning and the end, where the protection that comes through the holy spirit is treated, which teaches us faith through the pure fear of God. This fear engenders great amazement at the seemingly impossible work of faith. For the power of the All-Highest (which Luke describes in the first and last chapters) rejects all false, secret unbelief in the most radical way. This unbelief will be discovered through the putting on or breaking through of the divine spirit in the abyss of the soul. Paul says, 'You should put on Christ' [Rom. 13:14]. Then false faith can have absolutely no place. But whoever has not experienced this breakthrough knows absolutely and utterly nothing of faith. For he only retains his unexperienced faith in his hardened spirit, like an old beggar's cloak, which the false, doubt-producing scribes think they can darn most masterfully with a new patch, as the Gospel of Luke 5[:36] affirms. And for this patching, they employ nothing other than their stolen Scripture. If they are questioned as to how they came to such a high faith, since they so incessantly blabber about it, or why they would not rather be heathen, Jews, or Turks, or what kind of revelations they have had – since they so threateningly assail the world and so steadfastly defy it – then they come back with an infinitely insipid and stale smirk and simply say without shame: 'Behold, I believe the Scripture!' And then they become so jealous and hateful that they simply snarl straight out, saying: 'Oh ho, this one denies Scripture!' For, with their vices they most eagerly want to plug the snouts of all people. Like the fool – the pope, with his butter-boys – they merely want to appease the great unrest and the heartfelt suffering of the elect, or to assign this unrest and suffering to the devil, without any refutation. Our scribes, the learned clergy, usually declare that Christ rejected the godless scribes, so that one might think they are also similar to him. They stick out their forked little tongues and say in a soft way, 'Search the Scriptures, for in them you think you have eternal life and they are that which testify of me' [Jn. 5:39]. Therefore, the poor, needy people are so greatly deceived that no tongue can complain about it enough. With all their words and deeds our scribes make sure that the poor man cannot learn to read, because he is worried about his sustenance. And they shamelessly preach that the poor man should let himself be sheared and clipped by the tyrants. The scribes say: 'When will the poor man then learn to read Scripture? Yes, dear Thomas, you gush such nonsense. The scribes should read the beautiful books and the peasants should listen to them, for faith comes through hearing.' Oh yes, there they have found a fine dodge. He [Luther] would set up many more evil rogues to replace the priests and monks than the world has known since the beginning. God be blessed, however, that a great many of the elect recognize the root of unbelief where it has long been concealed. And, even today, this root would gladly like to grow wild, preventing the wheat from coming up. Therefore, shortly before the abovementioned words [of Jn. 5:39], Christ spoke to those 'pious' people, the scribes, 'My word does not abide in you.' And indeed why not? On account of unbelief, which will make absolutely no room for the true root of undeceivable faith, Matthew 13[:3ff.], Mark 4[:3ff.], Luke 8[:5ff.], John 9[:22], and Isaiah 6[:9f.].

Now, if such a harmful root is to be rooted out, one must be on guard against the godless ways of the scribes, with whom Christ himself in no way compromised. For they make a shameful cloak out of Scripture, a cloak that hinders the true nature of Christian faith from manifesting itself before the whole world, Matthew 5[:16] and 10[:5ff.].

The son of God has said, 'Scripture gives testimony.' But the scribes say, 'It gives faith.' Oh no, most dearly beloved, look much further about you! Otherwise you will have the most foolish faith on earth, like that of apes. In this way, the poor masses are seduced by the arrogant, itinerant scholars. Therefore, the concealed truth, which has slept for so very long, must once come to light boldly. And it must appear in such measure that, when a Christian speaks among the poor masses, saying he has learned the Christian faith from God himself, he would not be believed (as we are still today ready to believe) if he did not agree with Scripture in his account of the faith and that all of the elect should be taught by God, John 6[:45], Isaiah 54[:11f.], Jeremiah 31[:33f.], Job 35, and Psalm 18[:29], 25[:14], 33[:12–22], 71[:17], and 94[:10]. These and many other passages of Scripture force all of us to the conclusion that we need to be taught by God alone.

Now, if one has neither heard nor seen the Bible his whole life long, he could still possess an undeceived Christian faith through the correct teaching of the spirit, as all those had who wrote the holy Scripture without any books. And he could also be most highly assured that he has derived such a faith from the undeceivable God, and not from the image of the devil, nor drawn it from his own nature. Therefore, to gain this certainty, he must render an account of this faith, together with all its origins, before those people who also have a tested, uncontrived faith, responding to all their demands – just as gold is tested in the fire of the greatest sufferings of the heart. Otherwise a mere mockery and a completely flattering matter would be made of faith before the pampered ones, who have never once in their whole life seriously striven for true faith with the smallest thought. For they merely think that one should believe, like archseducers proceeding further with their fabrications.

Now, should we Christians unanimously agree, Psalm 72 [see, rather, Ps. 68:33], together with all of the elect among all religious divisions or every kind of faith (as the clear text of the Acts of the Apostles 10[:1ff.] gives testimony), then we must know how one feels who has, from his youth on, grown up among unbelievers and has experienced the right action and teaching of God without any books.

To this end, one should use Scripture so that one instructs with a friendly attitude each and every one, be he Jew or Turk, about such excellent works and the testimony of such people and teaches them how to judge which spirits are divine and which are devilish, 1 John 4[:1ff.]. Here our learned ones intrude and want to have miracles, as the godless scribes usually do, Matthew 12[:38]. With their too hasty judgment, the scribes give over to the devil the people who speak a single word against them, and they make a mockery out of the spirit of Christ. And they are so brazen that they dare to scream and write: 'Spirit here, spirit there. I praise my own writings. I have done it,' etc. And, so that they alone are acknowledged, they strive, day and night, with all their intrigues to kill those who say one word about the spirit of God. They do this just as the scribes did before they brought Christ to the cross. They said to Christ that he was not prophesied in the law of God.

And now our scribes say the same thing, indeed in a more perverted way. They say one should not take the spirit of Christ as the basis of faith. One should not even mention this idea. For whoever does mention it is marked with the first essential sign of a false prophet. Scripture (they say) should give faith. But the godless, pampered ones do not know any clear reason why holy Scripture should be accepted or rejected, only that it has been accepted by tradition, that is, by many people. The Jews, Turks, and all peoples also have such a greasy-ape way of verifying their faith.

But Mary and Zechariah, Abraham, Joseph, Moses, and all the patriarchs tell us about the opposite way of verifying faith, those who, in the abyss of their hearts, clung firmly to the stimulus of the holy spirit, and who absolutely and completely rejected the temptations of the desperate, unvirtuous godless ones, as Isaiah 8[:12] says. Thus, the agreed opinion and counsel of the godless describe the activity of the spirit of God as a disgrace.

The scribes speak as follows without becoming embarrassed: 'The holy Christian Church has accepted this and that. This article, this teaching is heresy.' And, nevertheless, they do not have the least inkling about real heresy. Nor do they know the least reason to justify why they are more attracted to the Christian faith than to any other. Therefore, the hireling clerics are such evil comforters of the poor, miserable, sad, heart-afflicted people.

SECOND

Each and every person should observe most carefully, and then he will certainly find that the Christian faith is an impossible thing for a man of the flesh, 1 Corinthians 3[:1]. Indeed, he will find further, everywhere in the texts of Scripture, that all right-believing people like Mary, Zechariah – Elizabeth, too, was one – found faith to be impossible. And it is also impossible for every sober, patient, serious, earnest, experienced person. Whoever pays attention to this will feel the hair on his head stand on end. Heed it precisely in this text of Luke 1. The angel spoke to the mother of God, 'For God nothing is impossible' [Lk. 1:37]. Why is this, my most dearly beloved reader? In truth, because according to nature bearing the son of God was an impossible, an inconceivable, and an unheard of thing, 1 Corinthians 2[:9], Isaiah 64[:3f.]. And all of us must have just this experience of impossibility in the beginning of faith. And we must hold to it that we carnal, earthly men shall become gods through the incarnation of Christ as man.[5] And so we will be pupils of God with him, being taught and deified by God himself. Yes, indeed, even more, we should be completely and totally transformed into him, so that earthly life revolves around into the heavenly, Philippians 3[:20f.].

Behold what an impossible thing this [deification] was to all the godless and the hesitant among the elect, John 10[:25ff.], Psalm 82[:5ff.]. They wanted to stone Christ to death because he spoke this message. Ah, dear lords, how meaningless the world will become when the voice of God reproaches you in the right way with the impossibility of faith and you must endure this impossibility until finally faith arrives, Psalm 40[:2].

So, why does Brother Soft-life and Father Pussyfoot [Luther] become so worked up and very angry, Job 28[:15ff.]? Indeed, he thinks that he would gladly like to direct all his intended desires into works. He would like to maintain his pomp and riches and simultaneously have a tested faith. The son of God accused the scribes of just this with clear words, John 5[:44], when he said, 'How is it possible that you can believe when you seek your own honour?'

Further, an additional impossibility concerning true faith is also set forth in Matthew 6[:24], with Christ saying to the disbelieving pleasure-seekers, 'You cannot serve both God and mammon.' He who takes these same honors and earthly goods as his master must finally be left empty of God for eternity, as God says, Psalm 5[:10]. Their hearts are vain, and, therefore, the mighty, self-centred and unbelieving people must be thrown off their thrones. Because, as soon as the holy and true Christian faith seeks to begin, with all its true origins, they seek to prevent it, both in themselves and in the whole world. Thus, for example, when the grace of God was announced through the birth of John the Baptist and the conception of Christ, Herod was ruling – that 'pious' blue blood that the nobility of this world dripped out of its sack, so that the most precious and highest good [Christ] could be clearly and easily recognized as the opposite of that godless one.

So, now, in our times, God also sends his light into the world. And this is proven by the government and authority of godless and nonsensical people who most arbitrarily and with all physical coercion rage and rave against God and all his anointed ones, Psalm 2[:1ff.], John 2[:16–20]. And these rulers have only now seriously begun to oppress and exploit their people. They threaten in this way all of Christendom. And they punish and blasphemously kill both their own people and foreigners in the most aggressive way, so that, after the struggle of the elect, God will neither be able nor wish to witness this affliction any longer. And he must shorten the days of suffering for his elect, Matthew 24[:22]. Otherwise, because the people lack time for proper reflection, they could not accept the incarnation of Christ and would become mere devils and heathen. And there would be more vexing sects than before the beginning of Christianity.

Therefore, Paul says, 1 Corinthians 10[:13], that God is so entirely true to his beloved elect that he does not impose more on them than they are able to bear, even though human nature always thinks that too much is put upon it. The good, omniscient father does not lay aside the rod of chastisement until the child has recognized his guilt, for which he has deserved this treatment because of the coarseness of both rulers and subjects.

What, most dearly beloved, is the source of this meaning in the Gospel of Luke? Behold, it stems from Herod, in whose reign Christ and John the Baptist were conceived and born, and also from what this text [Lk. 1:52] says without any ambiguity, 'He cast down the mighty from their thrones' – because, at present, the mighty take it upon themselves to rule the Christian faith, and they seek to set Christ up as a lord, one about whose advent they never have to think of preparing themselves. Nor do they allow anyone else to prepare himself for this advent. Nevertheless, our rulers want to condemn all people, and they want to remain the supreme authority, but only so that they are feared, prayed to, and held in honour above all people. And what is more, they always want to condemn the gospel in the worst ways they can think of. This makes clear the real art of Herod, the essence of worldly government, as holy Samuel, 1 Kings 8[:5–22] together with truly illustrious Hosea 13[:11] prophesied, 'God gave the world lords and princes in his wrath and he will get rid of them again in his vehemence.'

Since man fell from being a god to being a creature, it has become the most widespread commonplace to think that one must fear the creature (to one's own harm) more than one fears God. It is for this reason that Paul says to the Romans 13[:3] that princes do not exist to produce the fear that leads to good works, but to generate a fear of evil based on death. Therefore, rulers are nothing but hangmen and corpse renderers. This is their whole craft. But what is an evil work except that now one prefers a creature to God, and with awe and dignity? Oh, how did this come about? Because no one places God alone first (as is plainly evident), with his active strictness and all that he does and lets happen. Oh, the fear of God can and will not grow pure because of a greater respect for a human than for God, Psalm 19[:10]. Christ gave a very great and difficult command about just this, Luke 12[:4f., 8f.], and previously through Moses in Deuteronomy 6[:1–9]. In the same way, Mary also described the source of her faith (in order to support all the elect), saying, 'His mercy descends from generation to generation among those who fear him' [Lk. 1:50].

If the spirit of the fear of God is properly cultivated among the elect, the whole world will have to fear a righteous zeal for the majesty of God, whether it wants to or not, as David described in the first book of the history of the patriarchs, chapter 14 [1 Chr. 14:17]. But he who does not fear God alone out of the depths of his heart cannot be treated graciously by God, as each and every one learns from the contrasting words of Mary. Neither can we be saved by the hand of all those who hate us, nor can the heartfelt mercy of God enlighten our unacknowledged ignorance as long as the fear of God has not emptied us for the onset of unending wisdom. This is clearly written in Psalm 145[:19], 'The Lord does the will of the God-fearing,' and they are filled with this will in the wisdom and the understanding and the knowledge of God, Colossians 1[:9].

However, the world will not open its eyes to the source of faith. For this reason, all unenlightened people have to exhaust their reason with great, mighty efforts in order to serve a poor, miserable, wretched sack of gunpowder[6] and to shamelessly elevate it above God. Therefore, the world is too coarse to perceive God's judgment. Consequently, wisdom about God, the right Christian faith, has become such an alien, rare, hidden, unknown thing, and so completely impossible to attain that no eye can sufficiently lament and weep about it, nor can any tongue say enough about it. A dismayed man may not hear or read enough that the right, precious knowledge of God, the Christian faith, has been dishonoured and shamed. This has come about because those who are spiritless, who have no fear of God, have been assimilated into Christendom and must be publicly prayed to, as no one with eyes that see can deny.

Abraham in Gerar, as is described in Genesis 20[:11], ordered all his affairs according to the fear of God, through which the angel also recognized him, as is written in the same book [Gen. 22:11f.]. Abraham was infinitely awed, and where he did not act out of divine fear, he could not distinguish between the impossible and the possible. It was also the same for Zechariah and Elizabeth [Lk. 1:5–25], although they were righteous people before God and the world. They feared God above all things. Nevertheless, they could not distinguish between the possible and the impossible, because the spirit of the fear of God, which is necessary for the advent of faith, was not revealed to them. Thus, Zechariah could not believe the angel. Indeed, from the very nature of the case, this was to be expected. For his wife was old and besides she was unfruitful. It could not seem otherwise; she could never become pregnant.

Oh, dearest brothers, of what else does this Gospel of Luke remind us? Only that faith, with all its sources, presents us with impossible things, which the tender ones believe will never come to pass in reality. The whole insane, fantastic world sets forth instead a false path to faith, relying on glosses on Scripture, and the world says with a little forked tongue: 'Yes, one can indeed preach the Gospel, fear God alone, and yet also hold in honour the unreasonable rulers, even though they strive against all justice and do not accept God's word. Oh, for God's sake, one should be obedient to them in all things, those good Junkers.' Yes, welcome, you [i.e. Luther] defender of the godless! How fine, how very fine it must be to be able to serve with praise two masters who strive against one another, as the advisors of the rulers truly do! Oh, how skilful clever reason thinks it is! In its hypocrisy, it uses love of neighbour to dress up and ornament itself in the most imposing manner.

Yes, it is completely impossible in our time, much more so than at any other time since the beginning of perverted government, that the whole world can survive the force [of this contradiction]. Yes, this teaching of mine seems to countless people to be utter fanaticism. They can only judge that it is impossible that such a play could be presented and performed, knocking the godless from their thrones and raising up the lowly and the coarse [Lk. 1:52]. So they do not want to listen to Mary, although she is their most beloved Madonna, for they do not want to allow her to speak. Oh Mary, how can your words produce so much unhappiness in those who pray to you, those whom others want to rule. And yet, in an emergency, these rulers could not even bring order to a louse on their chest.

The world, and the untried scribes who are its top layer of scum, think that it is the most impossible thing of all that the lowly should be raised and separated from the evil ones. Yes, that is the true, weighty, and whole difficulty. The scribes do not want to give credence to the text of Matthew 13[:47–50] about the separation of the godless from the elect. From this text, they have imagined, visualizing from an old image of a scale's balance-beam, that angels with long spears will separate the good from the bad at the Last Judgment.

I think that the scribes could tweak the nose of the holy spirit himself. They shamelessly say that God does not reveal his judgment to anyone. Therefore, they deny that such angels, who are true messengers, will separate the good from the bad in the near future, as Malachi says [Mal. 3:1–5]. But our pious people, the scribes, cannot be accused of anything, as all can truly see, for they are 'impartial' – that means excellent arch-hypocrites who can easily bear the yoke of serving two masters on both shoulders. They speak, these highly credulous people, straightforwardly: 'No one can know who is among the elect or among the damned.' Oh yes, they have such a strong faith, which is so powerfully certain that it has absolutely and completely no understanding of anything except defending the godless. Yes, nevertheless, it is a fine faith! It will yet bring about much good. It will certainly produce a subtle people, as Plato the philosopher speculated (in *The Republic*), and Apuleius, the author of *The Golden Ass*, and as Isaiah 29[:8] says concerning the dreamer, etc.

The scribes cite St Paul, 2 Timothy 2[:19], to support their arbitrariness and to cloak their hypocrisy, as is their constant habit. They say, 'The Lord knows his own.' This is true, dear companion, but you must give up your piecemeal way of understanding Scripture and also give credence to the following words of the text [2 Tim. 2:19], which say, 'He who seeks the name of God avoids evil deeds.' A member of the elect may be a sinner, if he pleases. Nevertheless, he is guided by the consciousness of his sins if he merely perceives the sorrowful agitation of his heart, as Psalm 40[:12] attests. But the consciousness of the godless does not do this, as Psalm 36[:2–5] says. The consciousness of the godless strives constantly after vice and after greed and arrogance. No evil is too much for this consciousness. Therefore, it ultimately shows its real face. This consciousness can never be an enemy of evil, even though it, along with Judas, has a gallows repentance at Passion Week. However, at the bottom of its heart, the consciousness of the godless strives for nothing other than the same thing as the rich man in this Gospel of Luke 12[:16–21] – for a long and pleasure-filled life. And it always wants to have a good time. This form of consciousness thinks that it has been created exclusively for pleasure.

THIRD

One must perceive how the heart of a member of the elect is constantly moved to the source of his faith by the power of the Supreme Being. Thus, one of the elect usually says, Psalm 51[:5], 'Oh Lord, my sin is always before my eyes. Do not take from me your holy spirit.' For the spirit of God is most highly revealed through fear, so that the heart is completely and totally prepared for the reception of God's gift. For God cannot despise the repentant heart that has become humble. He must yield to it because such a good sacrifice is made from it. And this heart is redolent of the sweetness that, in its fulness, is most deeply hidden from many God-fearing people on account of their misunderstanding, Psalm 31[:10–14], until the time of a meaningful tribulation. Then, this sweetness is revealed to them, Psalm 34[:19], 1 Peter 2[:9].

Behold how Zechariah went into the temple [Lk. 1:8f.], according to the requirement of the law. This was nothing but that which is set forth in the Fifth Psalm [Ps. 5:7f.]: 'I will go into your house. I will pray before your holy temple in fear of you, so that you will lead me in the path of righteousness for the sake of my enemies.' Zechariah himself explained what this means in his present song of praise [Lk. 1:74f.], that we can serve God in his holiness and righteousness without fearing man. This takes place with an uncontrived, experienced faith that is very pleasing to God. Now, what is this faith in its clearest form? Each and every person should delve into himself and, in doing this, simultaneously perceive, on the basis of his turmoil, how he is a holy temple, 1 Corinthians 3[:16f.] and 6[:19] belonging to God from all eternity. Each person should also note that he has been created only in order to have the holy spirit as the teacher of his faith and to perceive all the spirit's effects, John 14[:26] and 16[:13], Romans 8[:14]. And each should also note that this same temple has been infinitely ravaged by ignorant parsons. Oh, every creature should indeed feel pity that no one wants to recognize such an outrage in the holy place. The poor people cannot attend to their hearts themselves due to the poisoning of the godless. Each one still stands outside the temple and awaits the time when it will finally be holy.

The common people think today – and have never thought differently – that the priests know the faith because they have read many beautiful big books. Therefore, the poor commoner says: 'Oh, they are fine men with their red and brown university berets. Should they not know what is right and wrong?' In truth, the people (even though they want to be Christians) have a foolish judgment, despite the fact that Christ commanded his followers most emphatically to distinguish the false from the true servants of God and to recognize each, Matthew 7[:15]. No one pays attention to anything except the accumulation of many earthly goods. Therefore, each one tarries before the temple and cannot enter into his heart due to his great unbelief, which he does not want to acknowledge on account of his preoccupation with sustenance. The holy spirit complains about this in Jeremiah [Jer. 5:4]. If, in addition to this, the people have completely relied on the parsons and scribes, then the people are dumb idols. They know much less of God than does an oaken block and a flint pebble. The prophecy of the Thirty-first Psalm [Ps. 31:18] is fulfilled, 'The lips of the deceitful become dumb.'

So Jeremiah runs around in circles, through all the streets, and would gladly like to hear a man who zealously applies himself to obtain God's judgment and faith. Jeremiah comes to the poor peasants and asks them about the faith. They refer him to the parsons and scribes. Yes, the poor miserable peasants know nothing about the faith after they have relied on the most poisonous people.

So the prophet Jeremiah 5[:4] thinks: 'Oh God, the peasants are hardworking people. They have spent their lives with the totally painful labour of obtaining sustenance, with which they have also filled the throats of the arch-godless tyrants. What, then, should the poor unlettered people know?' Jeremiah 5[:5] says further: 'I thought, wait! wait! I will go to the mighty ones. They will surely care for the poor people and bring them the faith and knowledge of God with words and deeds, like good shepherds. I will speak with them about it and without a doubt they will know.' Yea, yea, in truth they knew much less than the lowliest.

This is what the holy spirit prophesied through Hosea 4[:6]: the godless do not wish to have the right way to the knowledge of God available on earth. Thus, as the people are, so too is the priest, Isaiah 24[:2]. One blind person always leads another in this way, and both fall together over a bump into the ditch of unknowing corruption, Matthew 15[:14]. In this case, each one wants to puff himself up beautifully with the filth of another. And it is still the fault of all men that the whole Christian community prays to a dumb God.

Where else did this situation come from except that each peasant has wanted to have his own priest so that he has prosperity? At present, they do not wish it, for the whole world is not willing to help attain a good priesthood. Indeed, the world is accustomed to beheading good priests. Oh, a good priest's office tastes to the world like bitter gall. One must tell the truth. In relation to the nobility of our souls, we are much coarser than an unreasoning animal. This is because almost no one has an understanding of anything except usury and the other tricks of this world. When something is said about God, then the slogan of Solomon [Prov. 23:9] applies, 'If you preach to a fool, then at the end of the sermon he says, "Hey, what did you say?" ' It is just as if one addresses a sleeping man. So we poor, suffering, miserable Christians can express nothing about God except that which each has stolen from the Bible according to his own opinions. And, if the Bible were taken from us (which is possible), then one would be totally unable to help this coarse Christendom. Is that not the greatest misery? Yet no one wants to take it to heart. It is thought best that one remain silent about it. Oh, what gigantic, miserable blindness! Oh, that everyone has learned to see with but half an eye! John 9[:39ff.], Isaiah 6[:10].

FOURTH

If Christendom is to be truly made upright on another foundation, the usury-seeking scoundrels must be done away with and turned into the servants of dogs, although they can scarcely serve as such – and yet they are supposed to be prelates of the Christian church. The poor common people must nurse the memory of the spirit, and so learn to sob, Romans 8[:1–11], to plead, and to wait for a new John the Baptist, for a preacher rich in grace who has experienced every aspect of the faith through his own lack of faith. For he must know how an archunbeliever feels. And he must know that the measure of active desire corresponds to the measure of faith, Ephesians 4[:7f.], Psalm 68[:19]. If this does not happen, then this unexperienced Christian faith of our times will become much worse than the devil's blasphemy against God in the abyss of hell. Therefore, one must arise who shows people the revelations of the divine lamb in the form of the eternal word emanating from the father. You can surely see here [Lk. 1:21] that the people had an opinion about why Zechariah was in the temple so long. For the people could surely figure out and accept that, because of his long presence in the temple, he must have seen a vision. At that time, the people were not so absolutely and completely hardened as Christendom has now become through the evil scribes. In no way does Christendom want to believe that God is so near, Deuteronomy

4[:7], Jeremiah 23[:23], and capable of revealing his will to it. Oh ho, how shy the people have become about revelations, as Micah prophesied in chapter three [Mic. 3:6f.]!

Nearly everybody says: 'Yes, we are satisfied with Scripture. We do not want to believe in revelations. God does not speak any more.' What do you think? Had such people lived at the time of the prophets, would they have believed the prophets or preferred to kill them? Are they so blinded by holy Scripture that they do not want to see or hear how these Scriptures totally and powerfully insist that one should and must be taught by God alone? Should someone wish to be filled in another way than reading Scripture with the eternal divine gifts, then, after long chastisement through his suffering and his cross, he must be emptied for revelations, so that he may be filled according to the measure of his faith with the greatest treasures of Christian wisdom, Colossians 2[:1–3], Ephesians 4[:7ff.]. Each must receive the knowledge of God, the true Christian faith, not from the stinking breath of devilish scribes, but rather from the eternal powerful word of the father, in the son, with the enlightenment of the holy spirit, and thus be filled in his soul, in its length, width, and breadth, and in its depths and heights, Ephesians 3[:18].

In short, it cannot be otherwise. Man must smash to bits his stolen, contrived Christian faith through powerful, enormous suffering of the heart, through painful grief, and through an amazement that cannot be rejected. Through this, man becomes very small and despicable in his own eyes. The elect sink down while the godless arm themselves and mightily puff themselves up. Then the elect can raise God up and make him mighty, and, after experiencing heartfelt grief, the elect can rejoice from their whole heart in God, their saviour. Then the mighty ones must give way to the small people and be ruined by the small. Oh, if the poor rejected peasants knew this, it would be most useful to them. God despises the powerful and mighty, the likes

of Herod and Caiaphas[7] and Annas, and he accepts for his service the small, like Mary, Zechariah, and Elizabeth. For that is
God's way of working, and down to the present day he does not
act otherwise, 1 Corinthians 1[:26–9], Matthew 11[:25], Luke
10[:21].

Zechariah was a despised man since his wife was unfruitful. According to the substance of the law, Mary was equally
despised, Matthew 13[:55]. Oh, dear friends, they were not
mighty people with splendid titles, such as the church of the
godless now has, Psalm 26[:4–6]. Many poor coarse people
think that the great, fat, plump, chubby cheeks must possess
true knowledge about the source of the Christian faith. Oh no,
most dearly beloved. What can such people know who deny us
all living development of the faith and who damn and persecute
everything that opposes them in the most despicable way? For
they have consumed their whole life with animalistic gobbling
and swilling. From their youth on, they have been trained for
the gentlest ways, and they have had no difficult day their whole
life long. Yet they do not want or think of accepting a single
difficult day for the sake of experiencing the truth, nor do they
want to reduce their rents by a penny. And yet they want to be
the judges and protectors of the faith. Oh, you poor Christendom! How you have been totally turned into a chopping block
by your foolish rulers! How truly poorly they have provided
for you!

FIFTH

If the holy church is to be renewed by the bitter truth, then a
servant of God, rich in grace, must step forward in the spirit of
Elijah, Matthew 17[:3], 1 Kings 18[:1], Revelation 11[:3], and
he must bring all things into the right momentum. Truly, many
of these servants of God must be awakened, so that, with the

greatest zeal and through passionate rigour, they cleanse Christendom of godless rulers. First, the people must also be sternly reprimanded on account of their disorderly desires, those who so luxuriously while away their time without any steadfast interest in a rigorous consideration of the faith. Therefore, very few people know what to say about the first movement of the spirit. Yes, this initial movement is so distasteful to them that they have not even endured the ennui through which alone God's action is to be found, Psalm 40[:2]. In the first place, God's action is experienced through the sprinkling, Numbers 19[:19], where the waters of divine wisdom stir, Ecclesiastes 15[:3]. There the sad person perceives that God has begun a most rapturous thing in him. Thus, for the first time, he is terrified by God's name, which is revealed to him in the first movement of the divine action. He has no peace his whole life long, seeking this same name with his whole heart until he has received the grace from God to recognize that his name has been written in heaven from all eternity, Luke 10[:20]. Without this recognition, he can obtain no peace, joy, and righteousness in his conscience, even though they are due him, as is described in Romans 14[:17], John 17[:3], and Ephesians 1[:4].

Unless this happens, he stumbles after the true God in darkness and the shadow of death until his feet, after many attempts, are directed onto the path that leads to peace through the greatest discontent. All passions are directed towards this first sprinkling, caused by the blowing breath of the holy spirit, which arises from the deepest grief with the greatest groaning. If one expends all his efforts for this, then he can have no rest before the driving of the holy spirit, which never leaves him in peace in order to show him the way to the eternal good [God]. The holy spirit cannot make an insensitive person understand this except after the most coarse, foolish sins, for the coarse person comes to feel the gnawing, devouring thorns of his conscience without respite, as Psalm 32[:4f.] says. Then he must turn to

God and away from the sins and become their enemy. After all the pleasures of the flesh have been overcome, man must turn to God. Otherwise human nature cannot hold out. Then man first confesses his lack of faith and cries for the doctor [God], who on account of his solicitude can never neglect to help such a spiritually impoverished person. There is the source of all good, the true kingdom of heaven. Then he is first assured of his blessedness and clearly perceives that God, through his unchanging love, has driven him from evil to good through the sin by which unbelief is perceived. Then he has become completely liberated. This process is described in Jeremiah 31[:3].

Thus, true faith must win the victory, 1 John 5[:4], after it has triumphed over the world, a victory that is many thousandfold more abundant in the heart than externally. After such a rigorous recognition of unbelief, the exuberance of faith is no longer prevented from increasing in the person. Here you may weigh it and recognize, you literalistic fellow [i.e., Luther], how heavy your talent really is [Lk. 19:12–27]. But you cannot weigh it until you have at your disposal the scales of divine judgment for the examination of your heart, Psalm 119[:75]. However, if you want to make a mockery of the increase of holy faith, then you will be mocked, to your downfall and on account of your chubby cheeks, Proverbs 1[:24ff.]. How will faith be found? According to the scribes, one must only believe the Scriptures, without any discovery of the most certain witness of the spirit. And one should hide in the most covetous way of life, through which the godless hang onto each other like toads, as Psalm 55[:11f.] makes evident. No one can come to faith through usury and taxes and rents. The more that the shame of the world becomes longer and broader and deeper, the more the road is closed to human faith. Reasonable judgments are not to be disclosed in this way. If we do not improve ourselves in the near future, we will also have lost our natural reason, which we all still apply to the pleasures of the flesh because of our own selfishness, Psalm 32[:1], Isaiah 1[:4]. Thus, John the Baptist called the people who were on the side of the scribes a generation of vipers, Matthew 3[:7], Luke 3[:7]. For nothing but pure venom results when one preaches to lustful people. They select the worst things out of the best, just as later contemporary Christians have done with the precious faith.

It would have been better for them to have remained heathen with their forefathers. What is preached to them is said to the swine in the mud, Matthew 7[:6], 2 Peter 2[:22]. They run into the bog and are choked, Matthew 8[:32]. One may tell them as much as one wishes, or how they may yet obtain faith, but this is absolutely no help to them. They excuse themselves with their lame, insipid smirks: 'Yes, we are poor sinners. But if Christ did not despise sinners, how can this pharisaic spirit despise us?'

If I tell them about the faith that they have stolen out of Scripture, then they answer me with talk about sin in order to excuse themselves and to justify themselves with their appearance of faith and love, after which they deny the trial by God. For they do not want to accept the cure of blessedness proclaimed through the mouths of all prophets from the beginning of the faith. Therefore, they will be left empty, without faith and love, of which they have not a particle although they praise both in the most stately fashion. Since they can be such impressive hypocrites, everyone swears to the most holy that they are pious Christians. But they really are so full of all kinds of insidiousness that they thrust faith down on every occasion. How is it possible that one who is full of every lie can have divine faith, as the scriptural thieves seek to convince the whole world? Jeremiah 8[:8f.].

Thus, Christ was conceived by a pure virgin through the holy spirit, so that we might recognize the shame of sin in all its origins. For sin has come from our first parents through lust for the fruit of the forbidden tree, Genesis 3[:1ff.]. The human body has been disordered as a result of this. And on account of this, all bodily pleasures are also a hindrance to the working of the holy spirit, Proverbs 9[:13ff.]. All the days of a human life are nearly too short, Ecclesiastes 2[:1–11], to recognize this shame and to avoid it with rigorous renunciation. If someone is negligent in these matters and, with all his riches, wants to look like a prim man who has just vomited, and says without hesitation, 'Believe! believe! until the snot bubbles from your nose,' then that person belongs to the family of swine and not to mankind.

Each may gabble whatever he wants about faith. The lustful and ambitious are in absolutely no way to be believed, for they preach what they themselves have not tried. Therefore Christ says, John 10[:5], 'The sheep should not listen to the voice of a stranger.' The faith is foreign to the lustful and ambitious, and they to it, for they are far removed from salvation, Psalm 119[:155]. Therefore, they are also animals of the belly, Philemon 3[:19]. They preach what they want, but they still seek to fill the belly. Oh ho, to maintain their stomach they gladly take golden guilders with great devotion. They hardly need a hundredth part of what they take and nevertheless they want to be our evangelists. Consequently, their teaching also has no power, Matthew 7[:29]. Their teaching will be practised in absolutely no way except for the sake of the freedom of the flesh. Therefore, they poison holy Scripture for the holy spirit. One hears at various times that they walk along the right path. But that does not last long. None of them can improve himself, for their teaching is stolen, Jeremiah 23[:30]. In this way no one finds access to his heart.

John the Baptist, however, is a very different preacher, a confessing angel of Christ, who is represented in every true preacher. Each preacher should be praised, like John, not on the merit of his works, but on account of his rigour, which is born of persevering abstinence and which strives for a separation from pleasure, by which the powers of the soul are laid bare, so

that the abyss of the spirit becomes visible in all these powers.
For there, in the abyss of the soul, the holy spirit must persuade, Psalm 85[:9ff.]. For such a baring of his soul, a preacher
must be trained in a wonderful way, from his youth on, in the
withering away of his own will. Therefore, John was sancti-
fied in his mother's womb as a model for every preacher. Paul
says [Gal. 1:15f.] that John was ordained in his mother's womb
to proclaim the inestimable riches of Christ. For this reason,
preachers must know who always sends them out for the harvest, Matthew 9[:38], John 4[:35–8]. And they must know for
what harvest God has sharpened them, like a strong scythe or
sickle, from the beginning of their life. Not everyone can fulfil
this office. For, even if he has also read nearly every book, he
must first know the certainty of his faith, as did those who wrote
the Scriptures. Otherwise preaching is a thief's prattle and a war
of words.

SIXTH

What is never acceptable, accordingly, is the shameless defence
of false preaching by the malicious archhypocrites who want
to be kinder than God himself, insofar as they defend godless, damned, false preachers. They proclaim: 'A parson may
be good or evil. Nevertheless he can handle God's secret [the
Eucharist] and preach the true word.' These perverted defenders of the godless, indeed their companions (one raven does
not claw out the eyes of another), are clearly hardened against
the clear, ringing text of Exodus 23[:7], where God surely says
of a more insignificant matter, namely, worldly jurisdiction, 'I
am not well disposed to the godless. You shall not adorn their
affairs.' Accordingly, they violate still much more openly Psalm
50[:16f.], where it speaks of the ordination of the servant of God
and of his word, and God says to the godless preacher, 'Who

has called you to preach my righteousness? You take my attested covenant in your mouth and you have hated virtue.' And he would say today, 'Are you going to preach my dear crucified son to the world for the sake of your belly? Do you not yet know how one must become like him?' Romans 8[:29] 'You have not learned the knowledge of God and yet you want to be a schoolmaster to others?'

Therefore the totally abandoned person must be awakened by God from the desert of his heart. He must break out of this condition and strive to receive the truth among the lustful soft ones, who are really harder than diamonds. Through a tested life, he must have taken up the cross from his youth on, revealed it to others, and called out in miserable deserts to the erring hearts of those who fear God, since they now begin to seek the truth there, Luke 12[:36ff.].

Oh, these God-fearing people wish very much for the right faith, if they could only meet it. The desire of such people is described in Psalm 63[:2f.]: 'Oh God, my God, because of the light I have waited for you. My soul thirsts for you. Oh, in how many ways has my body struggled in the desert without a path or water. There I recognized myself and that I must experience your strength and praise in this way.' Thus, the power of God must be sought in the shadow of God. One may gladly rejoice over true preachers and that God wants to give them to the world in our times, so that the right testimony of the faith comes to light. Therefore, this text [Lk. 1:14] says, 'Many will rejoice on his account,' etc. The hearts of many will be disturbed on account of their negligence, which makes them persist in their unbelief. And they will reject this same negligence and exercise great care in the true faith through the unanimously discovered testimony of Christ.

You must always bear in mind here the whole context [of Lk. 1], one word after another, if you want to understand correctly what I say about faith and its impossibility. The elected friend of God discovers a wonderful rapturous joy when his brother

has also come to faith through the same process as he. Therefore, the mother of God gives testimony to Elizabeth, and she
in turn to Mary. We must do this as well. Peter and Paul con-
versed with each other. They discussed the gospel that Peter had
received through the revelation of the father, Matthew 16[:17],
and Paul had received through a heavenly disclosure, Galatians
2[:2]. But the poisonous black raven [i.e., Luther] mocks revelations, as you may see in his slanderous booklet.

In a short time, each will have to give an account of how
he has come to the faith. The separation of the godless from
the elect would indeed bring about a true Christian church.
What can the godless know of true faith, since they have never
been saddened by unbelief and have also never acknowledged
it? What, then, can they know of true faith?

SEVENTH

The present church, by contrast, is truly an old whore, one that
must still be judged with fervent zeal if the chaff[8] is to undergo
its separation from the wheat. But the time of the harvest is
certainly here, Matthew 9[:37]. Dear brothers, the chaff everywhere now screams that it is not yet harvest time. Ah, the trai-
tor betrays himself. The true Christians of the present time will
gain the correct momentum for change after every vexation,
Matthew 18[:7ff.]. For improvement follows vexation, after the
harm and the suffering of unbelief have reached their end. The
gospel, Matthew 8[:10–12], will be much more perfectly real-
ized than at the time of the apostles. Many diverse members of
the elect from many lands and foreign nations will be far superior to us lazy, negligent Christians.

Oh, dear lords, do not be so bold with your insane faith that
you give over all your subjects (excepting yourselves alone) to
the devil, as is your custom. For the profit-hungry evangelists

who hoist their names so high now begin to damn others to the greatest extent. They think that no one may be a Christian unless he accept their literalistic faith.

Behold how, in former times, Jewish comrades were lifted from the mass of the heathen: Rahab of Jerico; a woman of Salma from whom was born Boas, Matthew 1[:5]; Naeman of Syria who was brought to faith through Elias; Job was chosen by God from the Edomites; Jethro was brought to faith through Moses; Cornelius through Peter; a Roman official through our Lord Jesus, Luke 7[:1ff.], an official who was preferred far ahead of Israel on account of his great faith. The heathen woman was far preferred to the Jews at Jerusalem, Matthew 15[:21–8].

Even so, there are now many who will be chosen from the wild, strange heathen, to the shame of the false scriptural thieves. For, as I have heard from these heathen, they are astonished beyond measure at our faith, and they are held back from converting by our loose impudence. They are often perplexed by hyperrational afflictions and yet, as a result, are sure that they are inclined and ordained to eternal life, Acts 13[:48]. They lack only the true testimony of the faith, as do we all as well. Otherwise, innumerable heathen and Turks would become Christians. You can surely realize that if any Jew or Turk should be living among us and should be improved at all through this faith that we profess at present, then he would gain from it as much value as a gnat can carry on its tail, indeed much less. For there is no people under the sun that so pitifully hereticizes, damns, and dishonours its own laws as do present-day Christians. And especially the literalistic rogues are the leading cause of every evil, and nevertheless they still want to justify the whole world. But they do not even believe that God might bestow or grant them goods worth a penny. Thus, every corner is full of the greedy and the treacherous, Psalm 55[:12].

And those who should preside most supremely over Christendom, since they are called princes, supremely prove their lack of faith in all their actions and plans. And the princes also prove that they are afraid to do right before their fellow rulers, Isaiah 1[:23]. They think that they would be driven out of their principalities if they were to stand by the truth, which they have only accepted *pro forma* and only for as long as no persecution has befallen them. They also want to be called 'most Christian' and to strut about here and there, straightforwardly defending the godless and their followers. They do not want to intervene when their subjects are persecuted by their own vassals for the sake of the gospel. They want merely to be the hangers of thieves and good, majestic corpse renderers. The so-called pious people, the princes' parsons who preach the gospel to them, marry old women with great wealth, for they are worried that they might finally have to look for their own bread. Yes, truly, they are fine evangelical people! They surely have a firm and strong faith! Whoever relies on their plausible façade and on their prattle, with their monastic idols, will prosper. For they brag a great deal about this. And they puff up their literalistic faith far more than anyone can say.

I say to you, most dear brothers, it is not possible for me to be silent about this. I would rather instruct heathen, Turks, and Jews with the most trivial word, speaking of God and his ordering of creation, giving an account of God's rule over us, and ours over other creatures. For the most clever scriptural thieves fundamentally deny this, so that what Jude and Peter say in their letters [Jude 10:2, 2 Pet. 2:12] will become true for them too: 'What they know, therein they corrupt themselves, like irrational animals. Yes, they even repudiate it.'[9] They have neither sense nor understanding because of their insane faith. And they malign everything that they do not wish to accept. They want neither to hear nor see it when I admonish them in a friendly way to take up the Bible and learn about God's rule over us and ours over creatures. So, for them, all this is fanaticism. Therefore, I say that, if you scribes do not want to learn to truly take up the Bible, you will not understand and assimilate the truth concerning either God or creatures (to the praise of God's true name). And God will disgrace you in the most evident way through the heathen, who will prosper, so that those Christians who come later will spit on you, when you are even remembered.

If our scribes, along with their mortal idols [the princes], now want to snarl and fume mightily about what I say, they can nevertheless find their error in this Gospel of Luke by comparing it with the whole of holy Scripture. Jesus was conceived in Galilee, at Nazareth, and brought up in the same place, Matthew 3[:13]. The apostles have described it very exactly. So if anyone makes a synopsis to harmonize all four gospels, he will recognize this scribal error in the clearest fashion and not without excellent and powerful reasons, as anyone can see in the Gospel of John 7[:50ff.]. The rabid, furious, nonsensical thieves of Scripture believed in their carnal brain that Jesus of Nazareth could not in any way be the Christ, since he grew up in Galilee. They held to Scripture without the spirit of Scripture, as the godless ones down to the present day are accustomed to do. They punished poor Nicodemus due to his simple faith [Jn. 7:50ff.]. They referred him to Scripture and thought they had settled the matter. But God led them around by their noses. Consequently, they were not able to grasp Scripture in the context of its wholeness, due to their great blindness. And they paid no attention to the wonderful work of God, just as now our envious fantasts seduce the people to all kinds of presumptuousness, as anyone can see with his own eyes. But to prevent just this, holy Scripture was left to us negligent ones as our sole consolation here on earth.

If Scripture were not dear to the scriptural thieves on account of their bellies, etc., then they could certainly have known the time of Christ's birth from Daniel [2:44 and 12:1ff.], and from Micah [5:1] the name of the city that had been selected for the birth. And through Isaiah [7:14ff., 9:5, 11:1f.] and others they could have known of the coming of our saviour.

For the scribes then (as for the world now), everything turned on the fact that Christ was a lowly person, of unimportant parents. And nevertheless, he wanted too much to instruct and punish the mighty chubby-cheeks and the lustful people. He so clearly preached the wisdom of his heavenly father that the scribes could not refute it. And he worked such miracles that they could not reject them, John 9[:32f.]. Then one scribe said to another, 'Whence does he receive the wisdom and the power? He is a carpenter's son. Is not his mother called Mary? From where then could he receive all this?' And they were angry with him, Matthew 13[:55ff.], Luke 4[:22, 28]. The godless react this way down to the present whenever anyone punishes them for their façades, their pomp, and their false hair-splitting wisdom. Oh, how often has the eternal word concealed itself in the elect, in our Nazareth within Christendom – that is, in the burgeoning elect, who are renewed and who sweetly prosper in the wisdom of the cross. And every lustful pussyfoot has regarded them as crazy and nonsensical. This is the world's evil way. People anger themselves most about that which should improve them. Oh, most dearly beloved, this is the wisdom of the cross, with which God greets his elect. One should not anger himself over the condition of the world and see nothing good in any corner. And the whole world gets angry at the effect of the highest good and says that it is a diabolical apparition.

EIGHTH

The elect would be filled beyond measure with the grace of God if they immediately set aside their own will and made room for God's will. Christ says with clear words, 'Who does the will of my father there, he is my mother,' Matthew 12[:50], Mark

3[:35], Luke 8[:21]. For our sake, on the cross, he entrusted his mother to the care of his followers as our companion. Like her, we are also terrified by God's greeting, when God wants to deify us with the incarnation of his son and when he tests our faith like gold in a fire. We think, 'Oh, what is going to happen?' Mary was suspicious of the angel, in accordance with human nature, just as we are suspicious of acknowledging truthful preachers who explain and present to us the cross and the impossibility of faith, so that we recognize that therein is the true kingdom of David; there Christ rules from the cross, and we are crucified with him. There the house of Jacob [Lk. 1:33] is as well, the empty soul, emptied by the crushing of its loins – that is, by the removal of its lusts. There [in the cross] the power of the almighty brings forth the impossible work of God, in our suffering and through the ecstasy of the holy, ancient covenant. And God's power will be completely illuminated by the light of the world, who is the true and unfeigned son of God, Jesus Christ.

The whole of this first chapter of Luke is about the strengthening of the spirit in faith. This means only that almighty God, our dear Lord, wants to give us the most exalted Christian faith by means of the incarnation of Christ. God does this so that we emulate Christ in his suffering and life through ecstasy in the holy spirit, against whom the world rages in a bitter and carnal fashion and mocks in the coarsest way. Thus, faith will be given only to the poor in spirit (who also recognize their unbelief).

This conclusion is confirmed by every word of the whole first chapter of Luke, and especially in the most wonderful songs of praise of Mary and Zechariah, which speak so clearly of the heartfelt mercy that will be received through the spirit of the fear of God. This is the holy covenant which God swore to Abraham and to all of us, Romans 4[:13]. To keep this covenant, we should serve him in holiness and righteousness, a righteousness that God will also exercise over us. Whoever does not truly fear

God cannot be renewed from day to day in the knowledge of God. But this knowledge is necessary for man to understand the faith and the work of God in him. Nor can one who does not fear God learn to render an account of the faith. Because the fear of God is presently despised, faith is a rare thing that God will grant and enlarge only in tribulation. May the spirit of Christ, which mocks the godless, help you. Amen.

4

Highly Provoked Defence

Highly provoked defence and answer to the spiritless, soft-living flesh at Wittenberg, who has most lamentably befouled pitiable Christianity in a perverted way by his theft of holy Scripture.[1]

By Thomas Müntzer, Allstedter.

From the caverns of Elijah, whose zeal spares no one, 3 Kings 18 [see, rather, 1 Kg. 19:9ff.], Matthew 17[:1ff.], Luke 1[:11, 26f.], and Revelation 11[:3].

Written in the year 1524.

'Oh God, save me from the false accusations of men so that I may keep your commandments. And so that I may proclaim the truth that was born in your son, lest the stratagems of the evildoers endure longer.'

To the most illustrious, firstborn prince and all-powerful lord, Jesus Christ, the gracious king of all kings, the brave duke of all believers, my most gracious lord and faithful protector – and to his troubled, only bride, poor Christendom. All praise, name, honour, and dignity, title, and all glory are yours alone, you eternal son of God, Philippians 2[:9–11], because your holy spirit has constantly had the fate of seeming to those graceless lions, the scribes, to be a most enraged devil, John 8[:48], even though you possessed this spirit beyond measure from the beginning, John 3[:14]. And all of the elect have received this spirit from your bounty, John 1[:16], and thus it lives in them, 1 Corinthians 3[:16] and 6[:19], 2 Corinthians 1[:21f.], Ephesians 1[:13], and Psalm 5[:12f.]. You give the spirit to all who approach you, according to the measure of their faith, Ephesians 4[:7], Psalm 68[:10–12]. And he who does not have Christ's spirit, so that he can give an unmistakable testimony of it from his own spirit, does not belong to you, Christ, Romans 8[:9]. You have the invincible testimony, Psalm 93[:3–5].

So it is scarcely a great surprise that the most ambitious scribe of all, Doctor Liar, increasingly as time passes, becomes an arrogant fool and clothes himself in your holy Scripture, without his own name and comfort withering away at all. And Luther uses Scripture in a most deceptive way and actually wants to have nothing to do with you, Isaiah 58[:1ff.], as if through you he had attained the gates of truth to knowledge of you. And, thus, he is insolent in your presence and fundamentally he despises your true spirit. For he betrays himself clearly and irrevocably in that, out of raging envy and in the bitterest hatred, he mocks me, a member of the community that is integrated to you. He does this without sincere and true cause before his flattering, mocking, and most ferocious associates. And, before the simple people, he describes me in uncalled-for anger as a Satan or devil. And he slanders and mocks me with his perverted, vicious judgment.

But in you, Christ, I am blissful, and, through your mild comfort, I am totally satisfied, just as you also most sweetly told your dearest friends, saying in Matthew 10[:24], 'The disciple does not have it better than the master.' Oh, innocent duke and comforting saviour, since they have blasphemously called you Beelzebub, how much more will they insult me, your untiring foot-soldier, after I expressed my views about the flatter-

SERMON TO THE PRINCES **73**

ing rogue at Wittenberg and followed your voice? John 10[:4f.]
Indeed, this will always happen if one does not want to let these
soft-living people, who follow their own arbitrary opinions,
get away with their contrived faith and pharisaical tricks, but
instead wishes to see their fame and pompousness collapse. In
the same way you, Christ, were not accorded recognition by
the scribes. The scribes also had the illusion that they were more
learned than you and your disciples. Indeed, with their literalistic pigheadedness they were probably more learned than Doctor
Mockery could ever be. Even though they had reputation and
fame enough throughout the whole world, it was still not right
that they proceeded against you rationalistically and sought
to prove you wrong with clear Scripture, as they previously
rejected Nicodemus, John 7[:50ff.], and spoke of the Sabbath,
John 5[:9f.] and 9[:16]. They cited the whole Scripture against
you in the most extreme manner, arguing that you should and
must die because you freely confessed yourself to be the son of
God, born of the eternal father, just as we confess ourselves to
be born of your spirit. Thus the scribes said, 'We have a law
according to which he must die.' And they misapplied to you
the text of Deuteronomy 13[:1–6] and 18[:20] and did not wish
carefully to explore this text any further, just as the cunning
scriptural thief [Luther] now does to me. There, where Scripture reveals itself most clearly, he mocks with fervent envy and
calls the spirit of God a devil.

The whole of holy Scripture (as all creatures also prove) speaks
only of the crucified son of God. Because Christ himself began
to explain his mission or office [in the succession] beginning
with Moses and extending on through all the prophets, therefore he had to suffer in such a way [i.e., by crucifixion] in order
to enter into the glory of his father. This is clearly described in
the last chapter of Luke [Lk. 24:25ff. and 44–7]. And Paul also
says that he can only preach the crucified Christ, 1 Corinthians
1[:23]. After Paul searched the law of God more deeply than all

his contemporaries, Galatians 1[:11–16], he could find in it only the suffering son of God, who said, Matthew 5[:17], that he did not come to revoke the law or to destroy the covenant of God, but much more to perfect, explain, and fulfil it.

The spiteful scribes were not able to acknowledge all this for they had not searched Scripture with their whole heart and spirit as they should have done, Psalm 119[:2], and as Christ commanded them, John 5[:39]. They were learned in Scripture like apes who want to imitate a cobbler making shoes and only ruin the leather. Oh, why is this? They want to receive the consolation of the holy spirit, and yet in their whole life, they have never, as they should, come to the foundation of their existence through sadness of heart. For only in this way can the true light illuminate the darkness and so give us the power to become children of God, as is clearly written, Psalms 55[:2–9] and 63[:1ff.], John 1[:4f.].

If then Christ is merely accepted through the testimony of the old and new covenant of God and is preached without the enlightenment of the spirit, a far more badly confused monkey business results than there was among the Jews and heathen. For everyone can clearly see that present-day scribes act no differently than the Pharisees previously did, insofar as they, too, build their reputation with holy Scripture, scribble and spatter all their books full, and they always babble more and more, 'Believe! Believe!' And yet they deny the source of faith, mock the spirit of God, and in general believe nothing, as you plainly see. None of them will preach unless he is paid forty or fifty guilders. Indeed, the best of them want more than one hundred or two hundred guilders. And thus in them the prophecy of Micah 3[:11] is fulfilled: 'The priests preach for the sake of rewards.' And they want comfort, pleasant leisure, and the greatest prestige on earth. And still they boast that they understand the origin of faith! Yet they are driven into the greatest contradiction, for under the cloak of holy Scripture they upbraid the true spirit as a false spirit and a Satan. Christ also experienced this, as, in his innocence, he proclaimed the will of the father, which was much too exalted and irksome for the scribes, John 5[:16–18] and 6[:41f.].

You will find that things have not changed down to the present. When the godless are trapped by divine law they say with great lightness, 'Well, now it has been set aside.' But, when it is explained to them how the law is written in the heart, 2 Corinthians 3[:3], and how one must be attentive to its teachings in order to see the right path to the source of faith, Psalm 37[:32], then the godless one [Luther] attacks the righteous and drags Paul around with such an idiotic comprehension that even to a child it becomes as ridiculous as a puppet show, Psalm 64[:8]. Nevertheless, Luther wants to be the cleverest fellow on earth, and he boasts that he has no equal. Beyond this, he also calls all the poor in spirit 'fanatics,' and he does not want to hear the word 'spirit' spoken or even whispered. He has to shake his clever head. The devil does not like to hear it either, Proverbs 18[:2]. If anyone tells Luther about the source of faith, he is rejected. Thus Luther employs deception, 2 Corinthians 11[:13–15]. He sings in the highest register what he takes out of Paul, Romans 12[:16], 'One must not concern himself with such high things, but rather make them equal to trivial things.' The pap tastes good to Luther mixed in this way and not otherwise – but he dreads clear broth for breakfast.[2] He says that one should simply believe, but he does not say what is necessary for this. Thus, Solomon says of such a man that he is utterly foolish, as it stands written in Proverbs 24[:7], 'To the fool the wisdom of God is much too remote.'

Christ began, like Moses, with the source of faith and explained the law from beginning to end. Thus, he said, 'I am the light of the world' [Jn. 8:12]. His preaching was so true and so perfectly composed that he captivated the human reason of even the godless, as the evangelist Matthew describes in chapter

13[:54f.], and as Luke also gives us to understand in chapter 2[:47]. But, since the teaching of Christ was too elevated for the scribes, and the person and life of Christ were too lowly, they became angered with him and his teaching. They openly said that he was a Samaritan and possessed by the devil. For their judgment was made according to the flesh. As this false judgment pleases the devil in such circumstances, it must reveal itself as diabolic, for the scribes did not displease the worldly powers, who appreciate a Brother Soft-life [Luther], Job 28 [see, rather, Job 27:13–20]. The scribes did all they could to please the world, Matthew 6[:1–5] and 23[:5–7].

The godless flesh at Wittenberg does the same to me, now that I strive for the clear purity of the divine law, Psalm 19[:8–11], through the right approach to the Bible and the right ordering of its first part [i.e., the Pentateuch]. And I explain, through all the pronouncements of the Bible, the fulfilment of the spirit of the fear of God, Isaiah 11[:1ff.]. Nor will I allow Luther in his perverted way to treat the new covenant of God without declaring the divine commandment and the onset of faith, which is only experienced after the chastisement of the holy spirit, John 16[:8]. For the spirit punishes unbelief only after there is a knowledge of the law, an unbelief no one knows unless he has previously acknowledged it in his heart passionately, like the most unbelieving heathen. Thus, from the beginning, all of the elect have recognized their unbelief through the exercise of the law, Romans 2[:12] and 7[:6f.]. I affirm Christ, with all his members [i.e., the true church], as the fulfiller of the law, Psalm 19[:7]. For the will of God and his work must be fundamentally fulfilled through the observation of the law, Psalm 1[:1f.], Romans 12[:2]. Otherwise, no one could distinguish faith from unbelief unless he did so in a false way, as did the Jews with their Sabbath and Scriptures, without once perceiving the foundation of their souls.

I have done nothing to the malicious black raven [Luther] (which Noah symbolically released from the ark [see Gen.

8:6ff.]) except that, like an innocent dove, I have spread my wings, covered them with silver, purified them in a sevenfold manner, and let the feathers on the back become golden, Psalm 68[:14], and I have flown over and despised the carcass on which the raven gladly sits. For I want the whole world to know that, as you see in his pamphlet against me, he flatters the godless rogues [i.e., the Saxon princes], and he wants to defend everything about them. It is clearly evident from all this, then, that Doctor Liar does not dwell in the house of God, Psalm 15[:4], for the godless are not despised by him. Rather, for the sake of the godless, many God-fearing people are insulted as devils and rebellious spirits. The black raven knows this well. In order to get the carcass, he picks out the eyes of the swine's head. He blinds the pleasure-seeking rulers to their obligations because he is so docile and so that he will be as full as they of honours, goods, and especially the highest titles.

The Jews continually wanted to slander and discredit Christ, just as Luther now does me. He rebukes me mightily, and, after I have preached the rigour of the law, he throws before me the kindness of the son of God and his dear friends. I preached that the punishment of the law has not been removed for godless transgressors (even though they be rulers). Rather, I preached that the law should be enforced with the greatest strictness, as Paul instructs his disciple Timothy, and through him all pastors of souls, 1 Timothy 1[:9–11], to preach the strictness of the law to people. Paul clearly says that the law's rigour should visit those who struggle and fight against sound teaching, as no one can deny. This simple clear judgment is contained in Deuteronomy 13[:9–12], and Paul also renders it on the unchaste transgressors, 1 Corinthians 5[:1–5].

I have let this message go forth in print, just as I have preached it before the princes of Saxony, without any reservations. I have demonstrated to the princes out of Scripture that they should employ the sword [to punish evildoers] so that no insurrection may develop. In short, transgression of divine law must be punished. And neither the mighty nor the lowly can escape it, Numbers 25[:4].

Then, right away, along comes Father Pussyfoot [Luther], oh, that docile fellow! And he says that I want to make a rebellion, which he supposedly interpreted from my letter to the journeyman miners.[3] He talks about one part of the letter, and he stays silent about the most decisive part, namely how I proclaimed before the princes that the entire community has the power of the sword, just as it also has the keys of remitting sin. Citing the text of Daniel 7[:27], Revelation 6[:15–17], Romans 13[:1–4], and 1 Kings 8[:7], I said that princes are not lords but servants of the sword. They should not simply do what pleases them, Deuteronomy 17[:18–20]; they should do what is right. So, according to good, old, customary law the people must also be present if one of them is to be rightfully judged according to the law of God, Numbers 15[:35]. And why? If the authorities seek to render a perverted judgment, Isaiah 10[:1f.], the Christians present should deny this judgment as wrong and not tolerate it, for God demands an accounting of innocent blood, Psalm 79[:10]. It is the greatest monstrosity on earth that no one wants to defend the plight of the needy. The mighty ones do as they please, as Job 41[:24ff.] describes [the Leviathans].

Luther, the poor flatterer, wants to conceal himself beneath a false kindness of Christ that is contrary to the text of Paul, 1 Timothy 1[:7]. He says in his booklet on commerce that the princes should make common cause with thieves and robbers.[4] But in this same writing he is silent about the source of all theft. He is a herald who wants to earn thanks through the shedding of the people's blood for the sake of temporal goods – which God has certainly not intended. Behold, the basic source of usury, theft, and robbery is our lords and princes, who take all creatures for their private property. The fish in the water, the birds in the air, the animals of the earth must all be their property,

Isaiah 5[:8]. And then they let God's commandment go forth among the poor and they say, 'God has commanded, "Thou shalt not steal." ' But this commandment does not apply to them since they oppress all men – the poor peasant, the artisan, and all who live are flayed and sheared, Micah 3[:2f.]. But, as soon as anyone steals the smallest thing, he must hang. And to this Doctor Liar says, 'Amen.' The lords themselves are responsible for making the poor people their enemy. They do not want to remove the cause of insurrection, so how, in the long run, can things improve? I say this openly, so Luther asserts I must be rebellious. So be it!

Luther is totally incapable of shame, like the Jews who brought to Christ the woman taken in adultery, John 8[:3ff.]. They tested him. If he had transgressed the strictness of the father's law, then they would have easily called him an evildoer. But had he allowed the woman to go free without a decision, they would have said that he was a defender of injustice. In the gospel, Christ revealed through his kindness the strictness of the father. The kindness of God extends over all the works of his hands, Psalm 145[:9]. This kindness is not diminished by the rigour of the law, which the elect do not attempt to flee. As Jeremiah [Lam. 3:31–40] and Psalm 7[:9] say, the elect want to be punished with righteousness but not with wrath, which from eternity God has never possessed. Rather, a wrathful God springs from a perverted fear of God on men's part. Men are horrified by the rigour of the law and do not understand how God, after all the rigour, leads them through the deceptions of fear to his eternity. All those who, through original sin, have become evildoers within common Christendom must be justified through the law, as Paul said [Rom. 2:12], in order that the rigour of the father can clear out of the way those godless Christians who struggle against the saving doctrine of Christ. In this way, the just may have the time and space to learn the will of God. It is not possible that a single Christian can devote himself to contemplation in such a tyranny [as the prevailing political order], where the evil that should be punished by the law goes free and where the innocent must let themselves suffer. That is how godless tyrants justify themselves to pious people. They say, 'I must make martyrs of you. Christ also suffered. You should not resist me,' Matthew 5[:39]. This is an enormous depravity. Why the persecutors want to be the best Christians must be carefully analyzed.

The devil slyly strives to attack Christ and those who belong to him, 2 Corinthians 6[:14] and 11[:14], sometimes with flattering mildness, as Luther presently does when he defends godless rulers with the words of Christ. And sometimes the devil does it with terrifying strictness, in order to show his corrupted sense of justice concerning temporal goods. Nevertheless, the finger of Christ, the holy spirit, 2 Corinthians 3[:3], does not imprint this kind of rigour on the friendly strictness of the law or on the crucified son of God, who sought to reveal God's will through the strictest mildness, insofar as both kindness and strictness harmonize when brought into their proper relationship, 1 Corinthians 2[:6]. Luther despises the law of the father and plays the hypocrite with the most precious treasure of Christ's kindness. And he scandalizes the father with his interpretation of the strictness of the law by invoking the patience of the son, John 15[:10] and 16[:15]. Thus Luther despises the distinction of the holy spirit between law and grace. And he uses one to corrupt the other to such an extent that there is scarcely any true understanding of them left on earth, Jeremiah 5[:31]. He hopes that Christ will only be patient, so that godless Christians can truly torment their brothers.

Christ was called a devil when he pointed out the work of Abraham to the Jews [see Jn. 8:39–52] and gave them the best criteria for punishing and forgiving – namely, to punish according to the proper rigour of the law. Therefore, he did not abolish the law, since he said in John 7[:24], just before going on to chapter eight, 'You should render a righteous judgment, and not according to appearances.' They had no other basis for judgment than to hold as valid that which was written in the law and to judge according to the spirit of the law. Even so, with the gospel, transgression is to be forgiven in the spirit of Christ, for the promotion and not the hindering of the gospel, 2 Corinthians 3[:6] and 13[:10]. But then, through such a false distinction, Doctor Liar, with his scribes, wants to make me a devil. Luther and his scribes say: 'Have I not taught rightly with my writings and dictations? But you have brought forth no other fruit than insurrection. You are a Satan, and indeed an evil Satan, etc. Behold, you are a Samaritan and possessed by the devil.'

Oh Christ, I consider myself unworthy to bear such precious suffering in the same cause as you, however much the judgment of the enemy finds favourable, perverted support. I say with you, Christ, to the proud, sly, puffed-up dragon: 'Do you hear? I am not possessed by the devil. Through my office, I seek to proclaim the name of God, to bring consolation to the troubled, and to bring corruption and sickness to the healthy,' Isaiah 6[:8], Matthew 9[:12] and 13[:18–23], Luke 8[:11–15] and 4[:18f.]. And if I were to say that I would cease from this because of the bad name with which I am tarnished by lies, then I would be like you, Doctor Liar, with your perverted slander and viciousness. Indeed, at first, you could not do otherwise than quarrel with the godless. But now that you have succeeded in this, you have set yourself up in place of the scoundrels whom you have so skilfully attacked. Since you now realize that things might go too far, you want to saddle your name, since it is so bad, on another who is already an enemy to the world; and you want to burn yourself pure, as the devil does, so that no one becomes openly aware of your evil. For this reason the prophet, Psalm 91[:13], calls you a basilisk, a dragon, a viper, and a lion, because first you flatter with your poison, and then you rage and howl, as is your manner.

The guiltless son of God rightfully compared the ambitious scribes to the devil. And he left us, through the gospel, the criteria to judge them – by using his immaculate law, Psalm 19[:8]. The desire of the scribes was simply to kill him, for they said, John 11[:48]: 'If we let him have his way, the people will all believe in him and cling to him. Behold, they already run to him in great crowds. If we allow him to complete his task, we will have lost, and then we will become poor people.' Then Caiaphas came also, Doctor Liar, and gave good counsel to his princes. He had things well in hand and was worried about his countrymen near Allstedt. But in truth it is simply that, as the whole territory bears witness, the poor thirsty people so eagerly sought the truth that the streets were all crowded with people from every place who had come to hear how the service, the reciting, and the preaching of the Bible were conducted in Allstedt.

Even if Luther racked his brains he could not have done this at Wittenberg. It is evident in his German Mass how jealous he was of my liturgy.[5] Luther was so irked that, first of all, he persuaded his princes that my liturgy should not be published. When the command of the pope of Wittenberg was ignored, he thought, 'Wait! I can still salvage things by breaking this pilgrimage to pieces.' The godless one has a subtle head for devising such things, Psalm 36[:4]. For his plans were, as you can see, to promote his teachings through the laity's hatred of the clergy. If he had a true desire to punish the clergy, he would not now have set himself up in place of the pope. Nor would he flatter the princes, as you see clearly written in Psalm 10[:7–11]. He has interpreted this Psalm very nicely, so that it applies to him too and not only to the pope. He wants to make carrion renderers out of St Peter and St Paul in order to defend his princely executioners of thieves.

Doctor Liar is a simple man – because he writes that I should not be prohibited from preaching. But he says to the rulers,

'You should see to it that the spirit of Allstedt keeps his fists still.' Can we not see, dear brothers in Christ, that he is truly learned? Yes, obviously he is learned. In two or three years, the world will not yet have seen what a murderous, deceitful scandal he has caused. But he also writes, innocently, that he wants to wash his hands of the matter, so that no one will notice that he is a persecutor of truth. For he boasts that his preaching is the true word of God since it calls forth great persecution. It astonishes one how this shameless monk can claim to be terribly persecuted, there [at Wittenberg] with his good Malvasian wine and his whores' banquets. He can do nothing but act like a scribe, John 10[:33]: 'On account of your good works we do not want to do anything against you, but on account of your blasphemy, we want to stone you to death.' Thus, the scribes spoke to Christ as this fellow speaks against me: 'You should be driven out not on account of your preaching, but because of your rebellion.'

Dearest brothers, you believe it is truly not a bad thing that is going on now. Anyhow, you have no special knowledge of the matter. You imagine that, since you no longer obey the priests, everything is straightened out. But you do not realize that you are now a hundred – a thousand – times worse off than before. From now on you will be bombarded with a new logic deceptively called the word of God.[6] But against it you have the commandment of Christ, Matthew 7[:15f.]. Consider this commandment with your whole heart and no one will deceive you, even though he may say or write whatever he wants. You must equally pay attention to what Paul warned his Corinthians, saying in 2 Corinthians 11[:3], 'Take heed that your senses are not confused by the simplicity of Christ.' The scribes have applied this simplicity to the full treasure of divine wisdom, Colossians 2[:3], in violation of the text of Genesis 3[:3], where God warned Adam with a single commandment against falling into sin in the future, in order that he not be led astray by the multiplicity of material desires, but rather that he find his pleasure in God alone, as it is written, 'Delight yourself in God' [Ps. 37:4].

Doctor Liar wants to advance a powerful argument against me – how sincere his teaching is. And he maintains that this sincerity will lay everything open. Yet, in the last analysis, he puts no weight on preaching, for he thinks there must be sects. And he bids the princes not to prevent me from preaching. I hoped for nothing else than that he would act according to the word, give me a hearing before the world, and abide by his decision to act according to nothing but the word. Now he turns it around and seeks to involve the princes. It was a prearranged scenario, so that no one could say, 'Wait, do those at Wittenberg now want to persecute the gospel?' The princes should let me preach and not forbid it, but I should restrain my hands and refrain from putting anything in print. That is indeed a fine thing! Saying, just like the Jews, 'We do not want to do anything to you because of your good works, but because of your blasphemy' [Jn. 10:33]. And truly pious people have always said, 'Even if he swears an oath, unless he swears by the sacrament of the altar it does not count for anything.' This same trick the scribes used very often, Matthew 23[:18], Luke 11[:39]. Nevertheless, they were 'pious' people. Indeed, they did no harm – if you only believe that the weak must be spared being troubled.

Blasphemy could make no impact on the hearts of the Jews, as you can gather from the gospel. Likewise, good works did not concern them much at all, as is also true of Luther. Therefore God held up to the Jews the work of Abraham, John 8[:39]. But there was a cruel hatred in those Jews who wanted to have a good reputation with the people, just as Virgin Martin does now. Oh, the chaste Babylonian woman, Revelation 18[:2]!

Luther wants to deal with everything for the sake of the word. But he does not want to begin to justify or condemn my case with the word. He only wants to make a bad case for me among the mighty, so that no one follows my teaching because it is rebellious. Whoever wants to have a clear judgment here must not love insurrection, but, equally, he must not oppose a justified rebellion. He must hold to a very reasonable middle way. Otherwise he will either hate my teaching too much or love it too much, according to his own convenience. I never want this to happen.

If I were to instruct the poor with good teaching, it would be more useful than to get myself involved in a dispute with this blasphemous monk. He wants to be a new Christ who has gained much good for Christendom with his blood. And what is more, he did this for the sake of a fine thing – that priests might take wives. What should I answer to this? Perhaps I will find nothing to answer, for you have anticipated and defended yourself against everything (or at least you allow yourself to think so)! Behold, how elegantly you have sacrificed poor parsons on the butcher's block in your first explanation of the imperial mandate![7] There you said that the mandate should apply to the priests, etc., so that your initial teaching would not be brought to trial. Then, hypocritically, you were perfectly willing to allow the priests always to be driven out. Thus you would always have produced new martyrs and you would have sung a little hymn or two about them.[8] Then you would really become an authentic saviour! Naturally you would sing in your true manner, '*Nunc dimittis*,' etc. [see Jn. 8:54]. And they would all sing in imitation of you, 'Monk, if you want to dance, the whole world will pay court to you.'

But if you are a saviour, you must truly be a peculiar one. Christ gives his father the glory, John 8[:54], and says, 'If I seek my own honour, then it is nothing.' But you want to have a grand title from those at Orlamünde.[9] You seize and steal (in the manner of a black raven) the name of the son of God, and you want to earn the gratitude of your princes. Have you not read, you overlearned scoundrel, what God says through Isaiah

42[:8]: 'I will not give my glory to another.' Can you not call the 'good' people [i.e., the rulers] what Paul calls Festus in Acts 25[:1]?[10] Why do you call them most illustrious highnesses? Does not the title belong, not to them, but to Christ? Hebrews 1[:3f.], John 1[:11] and 8[:12]. I thought you were a Christian, but you are an archheathen. You make Jupiters and Minervas out of the princes. Perhaps [you think they were] not born of the loins of women, as is written in Proverbs 7[:2], but sprang from the forehead of the gods. Oh, what is too much is too much!

Shame on you, you archscoundrel! With your hypocrisy you want to flatter an erring world, Luke 9[:25], and you have sought to justify all mankind.[11] But you know well whom you can abuse. Poor monks and priests and merchants cannot defend themselves, so you can easily slander them. But [you say that] no one should judge godless rulers, even if they trample Christ underfoot. In order to satisfy the peasants, however, you write that the princes will be overthrown through the word of God. And you say in your most recent commentary on the imperial mandate, 'The princes will be toppled from their thrones.'[12] Yet you still look on them as superior to merchants. You should tweak the noses of your princes. They have deserved it much more, perhaps, than any others. What reductions have they made in their rents and their extortions, etc.? Even though you have scolded the princes, you still gladden their hearts again, you new pope. You give them monasteries and churches, and they are delighted with you. I warn you that the peasants may soon strike out.

But you always talk about faith and write that I fight against you under your protection. In this claim, one can see my integrity and your foolishness. Under your protection I have been like a sheep among wolves, Matthew 10[:16]. Have you not had greater power over me here in Allstedt than anywhere else? Could you not anticipate what would develop out of this? I was in your principality so that you would have no excuse [for failing to show your true colours]. You say: under 'our' protection. Oh, how easily you betray yourself! I mean, are you a prince too? What do you mean boasting about this protection? In all my writings, I have never sought the elector's protection. I have taken care to prevent him from picking a quarrel with his own people on account of the goat-stall and the Marian idolatry at Mallerbach.[13] He wanted to make incursions into villages and towns without considering that poor people have to live in danger day and night for the sake of the gospel. Do you think that a whole territory does not know how to defend and protect itself? May God have mercy on Christendom if it does not have as a protector he who created it, Psalm 111[:6].

You say that three years ago I was expelled from Zwickau and wandered about. And you say that I complained about much suffering. But look what is actually the case. With your pen, you have slandered and shamed me before many honest people. This I can prove against you. With your vicious mouth, you have publicly called me a devil. Indeed, you do the same to all your opponents. You can do nothing but act like a raven, cawing out your own name. You also know well, together with your unroasted Lawrence of Nordhausen, that evildoers have already been paid to kill me, etc.[14] You are not a murderous or rebellious spirit, but like a hellhound you incite and encourage Duke George of Saxony to invade the territory of Prince Frederick and thus disrupt the common peace.[15] But no, you make no rebellion. You are the clever snake that slithers over the rocks, Proverbs 30[:18f.]. Christ says, Matthew 10[:23] and 23[:34], 'If they persecute you in one city, flee to another.' But Luther, this ambassador of the devil, certainly his archchancellor, says that, since I have been driven out [of Zwickau], I am a devil and he will prove it with Matthew 12[:43]. And he has obtained this understanding of Matthew contrary to the holy spirit, which he mocks and about which he flaps his cheeks, Psalm 27[:12].

Luther makes a mockery and an utterly useless babble out of the divine word. And then he says that I call it a heavenly voice and that the angels talk with me, etc. My answer is that what almighty God does with me or says to me is something about which I cannot boast. I proclaim to the people out of holy Scripture only what I have experienced through the testimony of God. And if God wills it, I seek not to preach my own cleverness from my own ignorance. But if I do preach improperly, I will gladly allow myself to be punished by God and his dear friends, and I am ready to assume responsibility. But I owe nothing to this mocker, Proverbs 9[:7f.]. I will not eat the jay, an unclean bird, Leviticus 11 [see, rather, Lev. 1:19], nor swallow the filth of the godless mocker. I am only curious about your true colours. Since you are from the region of the Harz Mountains, why do you not call the secret of God's word a heavenly bagpipe? Then the devil, your angel, would pipe your little song for you. Monk, if you want to dance, all the godless will pay court to you.

I speak of the divine word with its manifold treasures, Colossians 2[:3], which Moses offers to teach in Deuteronomy 30[:11–14] and Paul in Romans 10[:8]. Psalm 85[:9] says that the word of God shall be heard by those who are converted with their whole heart and who strive to find in the teaching of the spirit all knowledge about the mercy and, equally, the justice of God. But you deny the true word and hold before the world only an outward appearance of it. You turn yourself most powerfully into an archdevil since, from the text of Isaiah [see Is. 40:2, 6] and contrary to reason, you make God the cause of evil. Is this not the most terrible punishment of God on you? You are deluded, and, nevertheless, you want to be a leader of the blind for the world. You want to make God responsible for the fact that you are a poor sinner and a venomous little worm with your shitty humility. You have done this with your fantastic reasoning, which you have concocted out of your Augustine. It is truly a blasphemy to despise mankind impudently [which you do in your teaching], concerning the freedom of the will.

You say that I want my teaching believed right away and forced on others, and that I do not want to give anyone time to reflect. I say, with Christ [Jn. 8:47], 'He who is of God hears his word.' Are you of God? Why do you not hear it? Why do you mock it and condemn what you have not experienced? Are you still trying to work out what you should teach to others? You should much more truly be called a crook than a judge. It will become evident to poor Christendom how your carnal reason has indeed acted against the undeceivable spirit of God. Let Paul render judgment on you, 2 Corinthians 11[:13–15]. You have always treated everything with simplicity – like an onion with nine skins, like a fox. Behold, you have become a rabid, burning fox that barks hoarsely before dawn. And now that the right truth is proclaimed, you want to upbraid the lowly and not the mighty. You do just as we Germans say [in the legend of 'Reynard the Fox']: You climb into the well, just like the fox who stepped into the bucket, lowered himself, and ate the fish. Afterward he lured the stupid wolf into the well in another bucket, which carried him out while the wolf remained below. So the princes who follow you will be defeated, as well as the noble highwaymen whom you set upon the merchants. Ezekiel renders his judgment on the fox, at 13[:4], and on the beasts and wild animals, at 34[:25], that Christ called wolves, John 10[:12]. They will all share the fate of the trapped fox, Psalm 73[:18ff.]. When the people first begin to await the light of dawn, then the little dogs, Matthew 15[:27], will run the foxes to their dens. The little dogs will not be able to do more than snap at the fox. But the rested dog will shake the fox by the pelt until he must leave his den. He has eaten enough chickens. Look, Martin, have you not smelled this roasted fox that is given instead of hare to inexperienced hunters at the lords' courts? You, Esau, Jacob

has deservedly thrust aside. Why have you sold your birthright
for a mess of pottage? [Gen. 25:28–43].

Ezekiel 13[:3–9] gives you the answer, and Micah 3[:5–8].
You have confused Christendom with a false faith. And now
that distress grows, you cannot correct it. Therefore you flatter
the princes. But you believe that all will be well so long as you
attain a great reputation. And you go on and on about how,
at Leipzig, you stood before the most dangerous assembly.[16]
Why do you want to blind the people? You were comfort-
able at Leipzig, leaving the city gate with a wreath of carna-
tions and drinking good wine at the house of Melchior Lotter.
And although you were [interviewed by Cardinal Cajetan] at
Augsburg, you were in no real danger for Staupitz the Oracle
stood by you, although he has now forsaken you and become an
abbot.[17] I am certainly worried that you will follow him. Truly,
the devil does not stand for truth and cannot give up his tricks.
Yet, in Luther's pamphlet on rebellion, he fears the prophecy
of his downfall.[18] Therefore he speaks about new prophets as
the scribes did against Christ, John 8[:52]. So I have used nearly
the whole chapter [of John 8] for my present condemnation of
Luther. Paul says about prophets, 1 Corinthians 14[:1–5], 'A
true preacher must indeed be a prophet even if he appears to
the world as a mockery.' How can you judge people when, in
your writing about the monk-calf, you renounce the office of
prophet?[19]

When you tell how you punched me in the snout, you do not
speak the truth; indeed you are lying from the bottom of your
throat. For I have not been with you now for six or seven years.
But if you made fools of the good brothers who were with you,
this will come out. In any case, your story does not make sense.
And you should not despise the little ones, Matthew 18[:10]. As
for your boasting, one could be put to sleep by your senseless
foolishness. It is thanks to the German nobility, whose snouts
you have petted and given honey, that you stood before the

Holy Roman Empire at Worms.[20] For the nobility thinks only that with your preaching you will give them 'Bohemian gifts,' cloisters and foundations, which you now promise the princes. If you had wavered at Worms, you would have been stabbed by the nobility rather than set free. Indeed, everyone knows this. Surely you cannot take credit unless you want once again to risk your noble blood, about which you boast. You, together with your followers, employed wild trickery and deception at Worms. At your own suggestion, you let yourself be taken captive, and you presented yourself as unwilling. Those who did not understand your deceit swore to the saints that you were pious Martin. Sleep softly, dear flesh. I would rather smell you roasted in your own stubbornness by the wrath of God in a pot over the fire, Jeremiah 1[:13]. Then, cooked in your own suet, the devil should devour you, Ezekiel 23[:46]. Your flesh is like that of an ass, and you would have to be cooked slowly. You would make a tough dish for your milksop friends.

Most dearly beloved brothers in Christ, from the beginning of the quarrel I have been wearied by the unavoidable trouble it would give to the poor masses. But if Doctor Liar had let me preach, or defeated me before the people, or let his princes judge me when I was before them at Weimar, where they interrogated me at the request of this monk, then I would not have had this problem.

It was finally decided that the prince [i.e., Duke John] would leave the matter to the decision of the strict judge [God] at the Last Judgment. The prince did not want to resist the other tyrants,[21] who wanted, for the sake of the gospel, to let the case remain in his sphere of competence. It would be a fine thing if the matter were remanded to this eschatological jurisdiction. The peasants would gladly see this happen. It would be a fine thing if everything were postponed to the Last Judgment. Then the peasants would also have a good precedent, when they were supposed to do the right thing. When it came to their judgment, they could say, 'I am saving it for the divine judge.' But in the meantime, the rod of the godless is their chief hindrance.

When I returned home from the hearing at Weimar, I intended to preach the strict word of God.[22] Then members of the Allstedt city council came and wanted to hand me over to the worst enemies of the gospel. When I learned this, I could remain in Allstedt no longer. I wiped their dust from my shoes.[23] For I saw with open eyes that they paid much more attention to their temporal oaths and duties than to the word of God. They assumed that they could serve two masters, one against the other. They did this even though God, most clearly, stood behind them. And God, who had saved them from the powerful clutches of the bears and lions, would also have saved them from the hands of Goliath, 1 Kings 17[:36f.]. Although Goliath relied on his armour and sword, David taught him a thing or two. Saul also began something well, but David had to bring it to a conclusion after a long delay. David is a symbol of you, oh Christ, in your dear friends, whom you will diligently protect for eternity. Amen.

In the year 1524.

'Sly fox, with your lies you have saddened the hearts of the righteous, whom the Lord has not deceived. And you have strengthened the hands of your wicked ones, so that they do not turn from their evil life. Because of this you will be destroyed and the people of God will be freed from your tyranny. You will see that God is lord,' Ezekiel 13[:22f.].

This should be translated: Oh, Doctor Liar, you sly fox. Through your lies you have made sad the hearts of the righteous, whom God has not deceived. Thereby you have strengthened the power of the evildoers, so that they remain set in their old ways. Thus your fate will be that of a trapped fox. The people will be free. And God alone will be lord over them.

5

Confession

The confession of Reverend Thomas Müntzer, formerly pastor at Allstedt and now found in the rebellious band at Franken-hausen, made voluntarily[1] on the Tuesday after the feast of Can-tate [16 May] in the year 1525.

1. He [Müntzer] does not want the holy, most worthy sac-rament [of communion] to be outwardly adored, but only [regarded] in a spiritual way; however he says this is a matter for the judgment of each.

2. He says that he gave the sacrament to the sick, and himself partook, in the afternoon after he ate [at midday], and also that he took the sacrament at night, at every opportunity. He took [ordinary] bread and wine and consecrated them.

3. In the Klettgau and Hegau regions near Basel, he proposed some articles on how one should rule according to the gospel. And he made therefrom further articles. The peasants there gladly would have accepted him [as one of their leaders], but he declined them with thanks. He did not cause the insurrection in those regions [i.e., in the Klettgau, Hegau, and Upper Swabia generally], rather the people were already in revolt [when he arrived]. Oecolampadius and Hugowaldus[2] instructed him to preach to the people there. He also preached there that unbe-lieving rulers make an unbelieving people and that, because of

this, there would be a [divine] judgment. His wife has the letters that Oecolampadius and Hugowaldus wrote him in a bag at Mühlhausen.

4. He says that [lords'] castles are very onerous and overloaded with services and other burdens on the subjects.

5. He says he said that princes should only ride with eight horses, a count with four, and a nobleman with two, and not more.

6. Present in his league or covenant [*Verbundnis*] were firstly the Allstedter Barthel Krump, a tanner, and Balthaser Stübner, a glazer from the same town. They began the insurrection with him. The official [John Zeiss] was also in the league, although initially he complained about joining it. The league was directed against those who persecuted the gospel. And the register, in which the league's members were enrolled, was in the possession of the two members Krump and Stübner mentioned above.

7. Reverend Tile Banse, a preacher at Sangerhausen, urged him to write a letter to the congregation there, that they should stand by the gospel and persecute those who are opposed to it. This he did.

8. He says that he spoke to Dr Strauss at Weimar,[3] where he appeared at the written request of Duke John of Saxony and others. At that time Strauss was engaged in a dispute with the Franciscans, and Müntzer was heard to say to the brothers: 'If the Lutherans do not want to achieve anything other than to cause trouble for the clergy, monks, and parsons, they might as well forget about it.' Since that time, Müntzer wrote against [Luther] to one Johann Koler of Mühlhausen, saying that if it is not too far for Müntzer to travel, he would indeed like to come to Mühlhausen and drive him out. Perhaps this happened because Müntzer wanted to be there.

9. The reason that he accused and reviled the gracious lord, territorial prince and count, Ernst of Mansfeld, was that Count Ernst's subjects complained that the word of God was not being

preached to them, it was forbidden them, and they were not permitted to go hear it [at Allstedt]. Müntzer commanded them all to denounce their superiors. If the word of God was not preached to them, he said that they should then come to him. He wanted to preach it to them himself, and they should not let themselves be prevented [from hearing it] by anyone.

10. The people of Mühlhausen let him into the city, and Johann Rode, a furrier, and the brandy-distiller near the church of Saint Blasius took him in.

11. He was at Mallerbach and saw how the people of Allstedt removed some pictures from the church and afterward burned the church. He preached that the Mallerbach chapel was an evil den and that the business with the waxen images which were brought there was a superstition, not something commanded by God. The hermit of the place was warned to move away, and this happened. Afterward, as already heard, the church was burned down.

12. Apel von Ebeleben's house was wrecked and plundered by the brothers at Mühlhausen because it was an onerous house, according to sundry articles that the brothers discussed, but which were not known to him. The articles in question are partly the 'Twelve Articles of the Black Forest Peasants'[4] as well as others.

13. The city council of Mühlhausen did not want to join the league, but instead relegated it to the common man.

14. Nicholas Storch and Marcus [Thomae or] Stübner of Zwickau were with Luther in a drink shop at Wittenberg, a place where Müntzer has also been. To refute Storch and Stübner, Luther told them that he punched the spirit of Allstedt [Müntzer] in the snout. But Müntzer was not personally present [at Wittenberg] at this time.

15. Reverend Gandolf, the hospital preacher [at Frankenhausen] formed a military unit and the people of Herringen and Greussen were in it.

CONFESSED UNDER TORTURE:

1. Heinrich and Hans Gebhart of Zwickau, residing in the Bundesgasse, and all their dependants are wool weavers, and they joined his association.

2. Reverend Heinrich Pfeiffer stated that one castle in every region was enough. The others should be destroyed.

3. He [Müntzer] pronounced sentence on Matern von Gehofen and the other servants of Count Ernst in the name of the common assembly, and he agreed with the sentence. And he did this out of fear.

4. He fled to Mühlhausen and took refuge there, since it pleased him there so much and it was a secure city. His principal supporters there were Hans Kule, who lives near All Souls church and the two people mentioned above, the furrier and the brandy-distiller near Saint Blasius.

5. He confesses that if he had conquered the castle of Heldrungen, as he and all his followers intended, he would have beheaded Count Ernst, as indeed he often publicly announced.

6. He undertook the rebellion so that the people of Christendom would all be equal and so that the princes and lords who did not want to support the gospel [and who refused to accept the league after being admonished to do so in a friendly way] would be banished or executed.

7. The principal members of the league at Allstedt were:

⎧ Barthel Krump
⎨ Barthel Zimmerman   all of Allstedt
⎩ Peter Warmuth
Nicholaus Rukker
Andreas Krump
Bischof zu Wolferode

8. It was their article of belief and they wanted to establish this principle, 'All property should be held in common' (*Omnia sunt communia*) and should be distributed to each according to

his needs, as the occasion required. Any prince, count, or lord who did not want to do this, after first being warned about it, should be beheaded or hanged.

9. Also members of the league were:

Hans Rodeman ⎫
Peter Schutze ⎬ in Mansfeld Valley
Peter Bahr   ⎭

Tile Fischer of Weymelburg

Tile Banse of Sangerhausen

Peter Rodeman of the same place.

The register of those who enrolled in the league was in the possession of Barthel Krump of Allstedt.

10. He also made a league among the youths, when he was an assistant teacher at Aschersleben and Halle. Among the members of this association were Peter Blinde of Aschersleben; Peter Engel, a churchman of Halle; and Hans Buttener and Cuntz Sander of Halle, who lived at Stone Gate.

This league was directed against Bishop Ernst [of Magdeburg], of highly praised memory.

11. If all had gone as he intended and planned – it was his opinion and publicly known by all the commoners of his association – he wanted to occupy the land up to a forty-six-mile radius around Mühlhausen and to occupy the territory of Hesse, and he would have dealt with the princes and lords as indicated above. The majority of the league's members knew this well.

12. The people of Mühlhausen lent him eight artillery pieces. Count Bodo of Stolberg lent those at Frankenhausen a small field piece.

6

Selected Letters

May salvation and God's constant, eternal mercy be with you, my most dearly beloved brothers. I beg you not to get angry on account of my expulsion,[1] for, in such tribulation the abyss of the soul is cleansed, so that it is increasingly enlightened and recognized as worthy of obtaining the insuperable witness of the holy spirit. In order to discover God's mercy, one must be forsaken, as Isaiah clearly [testifies] in chapters 28[:19] and 54[:7]: 'For a brief moment I forsook you and in great mercy I have gathered you.' This is also what Christ, our saviour, says about this [Jn. 16:7]: 'If I go away, the consoler will come, the holy spirit,' who can only be given to those without consolation.

Thus let my suffering be a model for your own. Let all the tares bloom as they will; they must pass under the thresher with the pure wheat. The living God makes his scythe so sharp in me that, afterward, I will be able to cut the red corn roses and the little blue flowers.[2]

With this [letter] I give you my greeting. Be commended to God. Let he who is able share with me the wages of the gospel: 'The labourer is worth his wages,' Matthew 10[:10]. He who gets angry over this should give me nothing. It would be better to die than to besmirch the honour of God with sustenance that is given in anger. The whole winter I have had only two guilders, which I got from the abbess. Of these, I gave one to the youth [Ambrosius Emmen],[3] the second, and more, I owe on a debt. This youth is faithful to me.

Written in the misery of my persecution on the day of St Joseph [19 March] in the year of Christ 1523.

Thomas Müntzer, a willing messenger of God.

TO COUNT ERNST OF MANSFELD. ALLSTEDT, 22 SEPTEMBER 1523. (#44)

Written in a Christian way to the noble, wellborn count, Lord Ernst of Mansfeld and Heldrungen.[4]

Greetings, noble, wellborn count. The official [John Zeiss] and the council of Allstedt have shown me your letter, according to which I am said to have accused you of being a heretical rogue and an oppressor. This is true to the following extent. I definitely know, and it is common knowledge in the territory, that you have brutally ordered your subjects, by public mandate, not to attend my 'heretical' Mass or sermons. To this I have said, and wish to complain about it to all Christian people, that you are exceedingly audacious in allowing yourself to forbid the holy gospel. And if you persist (may God prevent this) in such raging and senseless prohibiting, then, from this day on, as long as my heart beats, I will not only describe you [as a heretical rogue and oppressor] before Christendom, but also I will let my writings against you be translated often into many languages. And I will denounce you to the Turks, heathen, and Jews as a foolish, stupid person. I will proclaim this and put it on paper. You should also know that when it comes to such mighty and righteous causes, I do not fear the whole world. Christ raised the hue and cry about those who take away the key to the knowledge of God, Luke 11[:52]. But the key to the knowledge of God is that people are so ruled that they learn to fear God alone, Romans 13, for the beginning of true Christian wisdom is the fear of the Lord.

But since you want to be feared more than God – as I can prove from your actions and mandate – you are the one who takes away the key to the knowledge of God, who forbids people from going to church, and who is incapable of improvement. In performing the liturgy and the preaching that I have undertaken here, I will support what I say with the holy Bible, even in the smallest matters that I recite or say. If I am not able to do this, then I am ready to lose body and life and all worldly goods. But if you are incapable of any reply except violence, then may you abstain from this, for the sake of God. And if you persist, like often before, in your persecution, then you should not forget a future of conflict without end. The prophet says, 'No violence or intrigue help against the Lord.' I am a servant of God just as much as you, so go gently in what the whole world must bear patiently! Do not make boastful trouble, otherwise the old garment will tear. If you force me to publish against you, I will give you a hundred thousand times more trouble than Luther gave the pope. Be my gracious lord, if you can bear and suffer it; if not, I will let God be my ruler. Amen.

Written at Allstedt on the day of St Maurice [22 September], in the year 1523.

Thomas Müntzer, a disturber of the unfaithful.

TO FREDERICK THE WISE. ALLSTEDT, 4 OCTOBER 1523. (#45)

To the most illustrious, highly born prince and lord, Frederick, elector and high marshal of the Holy Roman Empire, duke of

Saxony, count of Doringen, and margrave of Meissen, my most gracious lord.[5]

Jesus, the son of God.

Most illustrious, highly born prince and lord, may the righteous fear of God and the peace that is alien to the world be with you, your electoral grace. Most gracious lord, since almighty God has made me a resolute preacher, I have tried to blow the [Lord's] loud, moving trumpets, so that they resound with zeal for the knowledge of God, and to spare no man on earth who strives against the word of God, as God himself commanded through the prophet Isaiah 58[:1]. Therefore my name (as is self-evident) must necessarily be most awful, ugly, and useless to the clever ones of the world, Matthew 5[:11], Luke 6[:22]. To the poor, needy masses, my name is a sweet smell of life, but to lustful people it is a displeasing abomination of swift corruption, 2 Corinthians 2[:15]. And my life verifies that fervent zeal for the sake of poor, miserable, pitiable Christendom has consumed me. So the abuse of the godless has often fallen on me, Psalm 69[:10], has unjustly driven me from one city to another, Matthew 23[:24], and has mocked my response [to this abuse] most hatefully, Jeremiah 20[:7f.].

As a result of all this, I have thought day and night, Psalm 1[:2], about how I can cast myself as an iron wall for the [protection of the] needy, Jeremiah 1[:18], Ezekiel 13[:5]. And I have seen that Christendom cannot be saved from the mouth of the raging lion unless the ringing, pure word of God is brought forth, putting aside the bushel or cover with which it has been concealed, Matthew 5[:15], so that biblical truth is openly discussed throughout the whole world, Matthew 10[:27], testifying to both the humble and the mighty, Acts 26[:22], presenting to the world only Christ the crucified, 1 Corinthians 1[:17ff.], and singing and preaching [the truth] in an undisguised and indefatigable way. Performing my office of preaching so that the time does not pass in vain, but rather so that the people are edified with psalms and hymns of praise, Ephesians 5[:19] and 1 Corinthians 14[:15], provides proof for the basis of the German liturgy.

All my reasonable reproaches have been of no help to me and have not prevented the wellborn Count Ernst of Mansfeld, through the whole summer and thereafter, from constantly forbidding his subjects [from coming to Allstedt], even before the emperor's mandate was published. And, through this prohibition, he has caused our people and his to revolt. Since, in the long run, I could not prevent this rebellion through my efforts to persuade [the people otherwise], on the Sunday after the birth of the Virgin [15 September 1523], I pleadingly warned him publicly from the pulpit and eagerly invited him to visit my flock, saying: 'I bid Count Ernst of Mansfeld to appear here – with the clergy of the bishop – and to prove that my teaching or liturgy is heretical. But if he fails in this (may God prevent this), then I will regard him as an evildoer, a rascal, a rogue, a Turk, and a heathen. And I will prove this with the truth of Scripture.' This is exactly what I said, and nothing else, as I can prove.

He has treated me improperly, and now he refers to the imperial mandate, as though his affair was included in it, although it is evident that it is not.[6] He should have brought his learned ones with him and instructed me kindly and modestly. Had I been defeated [in debate with them], then he should have accused me before your electoral grace and, only then, forbidden his subjects from attending my services. If it becomes acceptable to stop the gospel with human commands, Isaiah 29[:13], Matthew 15[:7ff.], and Titus 1[:14ff.] – and if, in addition, the language of the mandate is not formally observed – this will drive the people crazy. For the people should love princes more than fear them. Romans 13[:3f.]: Princes do not frighten the pious. And if it turns out that [the princes do make the pious fear them], then the sword will be taken from them and given to the ardent masses in order to defeat the godless, Daniel 7[:18]. Then that noble treasure, peace, will be removed from the earth, Revelation 6[:2]: 'He who rides the white horse will triumph, and this is not fitting.' Oh, highborn, gracious elector, much zeal is necessary here, until our saviour, at the right hand of God on the day of his wrath (when he shall tend the sheep himself and drive the wild animals from the flock), mercifully destroys the kings, Psalm 110[:5], Ezekiel 34[:10]. Oh, may it please God that this destruction is not caused by our negligence.

I have not wanted to conceal this from your electoral grace with a long speech, Ezekiel 3[:17ff.]. And I greatly exhort you with an additional request – that you look favorably on my letter and allow me to be examined according to divine law [in order to determine] whether I am righteous in my defence. If I should now yield, my conscience and my conduct could not stand before Christendom, 1 Timothy 3[:9f.]. Your Electoral Grace must also be bold in this matter. Do you not see that, from the beginning, God has stood unceasingly by your Electoral Grace? May God protect you and your people forever. Amen.

Written at Allstedt in the year of our Lord 1523, on the day of St Francis [4 October].

Thomas Müntzer of Stolberg, a servant of God.

TO THE GOD-FEARING AT SANGERHAUSEN.
ALLSTEDT, 15 JULY 1524. (#53)[7]

I, Thomas Müntzer, wish all the God-fearing people at Sangerhausen peace, to which the untested world is an enemy. Since God's undeceivable mercy has blessed you with true preachers and instructed you, you should not let yourselves be led into error by the manifold blabbering of the godless. You should not lose heart and not completely become children, as Paul described for the elect and warned them from his heart, Ephesians 4[:14].

Pay attention that you are not led around by the nose with empty threats and with the cunning of greedy people. For it is surely true that they are all worried that the time will once come when judgment will be pronounced on them. And they have never once dreamed of this, never once considered it, and also never intend to consider it. Therefore, you should not be frightened by a ghost, Psalm 118. Let the message of God be held before you in the fear of God, as is written, Psalm 119[:38]: 'Establish your word unto your servant who is devoted to your fear.' Then all the mistrust of your unbelief will fall away. Then you will find that you must preserve God's judgment in this way: by the instruction and the dying of your heart. But if you truly want to fear God, this must occur by endangering the things we fear on earth through the presumptuousness of our unbelieving nature's fleshly understanding. God's goodness must move you to this, which now has such a rich stock that more than thirty groups and organizations of the elect have been made.[8] In all territories, the play is about to go on. In short, we are in a situation that we must see through to the end.

Do not let your hearts sink, as happened to all the tyrants, Numbers 24[:17–19]. It is God's proper judgment that the tyrants are so fully and miserably hardened, for God wants to tear them out by the roots. Joshua 11[:20] has prophesized this for us. Fear only God, your Lord, then the fear is pure, Psalm 19[:10ff.]. Then your faith is tested like gold in the fire, 1 Peter 1[:7]. There you will find so much wisdom that all our opponents cannot withstand it. I have often greatly wondered why Christians have more fear of tyrants than every other nation, and yet they see before their eyes how every attack of the godless at every moment is ruined. This is the product of unbelief and of useless preachers. So do not let courageous preachers be taken away from you, or you will value over God a poor, miserable, wretched sack of gunpowder. And you will not risk your body, goods, and honour for God's sake. And then you will lose everything you have for the sake of the devil. Pay attention to this – God will not abandon you. At first it will be hard for you, before you are able to suffer a little grief for God's sake. But you can be enlightened in no other way than through great grief, John 16[:20f.].

Out of brotherly duty, I have not been able to suppress this message of instruction and consolation. If something happens to you, my pen preaching, reciting, and speaking will not be far from you. Take heart! The godless rogues are already faint-hearted because of God's justice, which will strengthen you in Jesus Christ our Lord. Amen.

Written at Allstedt on the Friday after the feast of St Margaret [15 July] in the year 1524.

TO JOHN ZEISS, OFFICIAL OF ELECTORAL SAXONY. ALLSTEDT, 22 JULY 1524. (#57)

To his dear brother in Christ, John Zeiss, electoral official at Allstedt.

I offer you the true undeceived fear of God. Today I wanted to anticipate the filth of the widespread revulsion and to let you know about future treachery, in order to avoid any liability for it and to present the territorial princes with your counsel, so that no one is given improper cause [for violence]. I do this since nearly all the tyrants are actively engaged in persecuting the Christian faith.

Hans Reichart[9] gave the poor refugees [from this persecution] an improper answer, one according to the old customary law of the officials of the princes and their attendants. Then the exiles and the refugees asked me what kind of a gospel we have [at Allstedt]? Whether we were going to sacrifice on the butcher's block and in the most miserable way those people who were willing to suffer for the sake of the Christian faith?

Then I said that I have not been informed in any way [of their fate]; if I knew about it, I would gladly do as much as I could [for them]. Just then, as I was talking to the refugees, Hans Reichart came to me from the print shop. Then I said, 'What kind of a game is this supposed to be? Do you want to console the people who have been driven out on account of the gospel in this way? Can you not see any more clearly what kind of a game will develop?' Then he said that you ordered him to do it. If an official from Sangerhausen or elsewhere visited Allstedt, the people would have to be handed over to him. Then I replied that this would be just only if rulers didn't persecute the Christian faith. But since they were violating not only the faith but also these people's natural rights, they should be strangled like dogs. And if you officials in every district will not openly complain that your colleague at Schönewerda[10] was the first one to break the common peace and become a robber of his own subjects, then you will soon see what will happen to you. Thus I advise you, my dear brother, to consider well what will happen. Refugees will arrive every day. Should we please the tyrants with the cries of poor people? This does not line up well with the gospel, etc. I tell you that the terrible phenomenon of civil war will be unleashed.

You must no longer hold to the custom of obeying other officials. For it is as clear as the light of day that they think absolutely and completely nothing of the Christian faith. Their power has an end, and it will soon be handed over to the common people. So act carefully. Where the gospel is accepted, Christians are not imprisoned at the pleasure of rogues. I will stick sincerely and willingly to what I promised with my own hand to the prince.[11] But truthfully, I do not want there to be any tricks. Wherever the spirit of God compels me, in Christian faith, I shall endure the rulers as my judges. But if they have ordered you to arrest people who are refugees on account of the gospel, and if I knew this in fact to be the case, then I would renounce what I have written to him. I advise you to write the princes yourself (however trivial it may well be to them) about the archrobber, Friedrich von Witzleben, and tell them that he violated the common peace, and so he is an archetype of pure tyranny and the source of all revolt.[12] If he is not punished for this by the other lords, then the common peace will also collapse. For from now on, no people will believe in their own lord. And then the people cannot help the lord, nor the lord the people. Here perceptive and modest people can see the cause of all manslaughter made so pitifully evident that their heart justly trembles in fear. The insane world still mocks this; it thinks things are still as they were in the old life. The insane world always goes around in its dreams, until water is dashed over its head. Dear brother, may God protect you from this. Amen.

Written at Allstedt on the day of Mary Magdalene [22 July] in the year of our Lord 1524.

Thomas Müntzer, your brother.

[P.S.] Whoever wants to be a stone of the new church should risk his neck, otherwise the masons will reject him. Consider this, dear brother – whoever, in these dangerous times, is not willing to risk his neck, also will not test his faith. He will disparage everything so that he does not have to suffer. Therefore, he will have to bear much danger for the sake of the devil, be ruined in the eyes of all the elect, and finally die at the will of the devil. May God protect you from this. Amen.

With this message I wanted to deliver my pamphlet, which perhaps you recently passed on [to the court] at Weimar.[13] I always consider matters more according to God's honour and will [than man's], for it is now the most dangerous thing to act before those who mock the judgment of God.

In answer to your four questions:

1. The will of God is the whole above all its parts. To know the knowledge of God and his judgment is the explanation of this same will (as Paul wrote to the Colossians 1[:9], and as Psalm 119 says). But the action of God flows from the whole and all its parts.

2. Doubt is the water, the motion to good and evil. Whoever swims in the water without a saviour is between life and death, etc. But the hope that is attained after the action of doubt best confirms the person, Romans 4[:18ff.], Genesis 13[:15f.] and 22[:12,17f.].

3. You have grasped well the judgment about the essential quality of a person, but first the coarse conditions must all be consumed before the person can begin to control his nature. Otherwise a person always goes around with a deceptive appearance, and also deceives himself. Therefore, one must see to it, if he is inclined to unchastity, that he hurts his lust the very first time he sins, by making a determined effort to observe both his lust and the thorns of his conscience. If he keeps his conscience active, then the filth of unchastity consumes itself in horror. In this state of mind, one sees clearly everything that moves a person to filth, to which one becomes an enemy – and first of all an enemy of lust through ennui. When this indifference frustrates him, then he fails again, so that he is again driven by conscience. A person who remains quiet will be easily enlightened.

4. A person cannot come to the first true Christian memory without suffering, for the heart must be torn from clinging to this world through laments and pains, until one is absolutely and completely an enemy to this life. Whoever has attained this is able to generate more good days than bad with a secure conscience, something which is clearly announced in the Gospel of John [Jn. 21:21], and by Elias [2 Kg. 2:11], and by Enoch [Gen. 5:24].

Lastly, in the deplorable, current state of affairs, there remains only this – the refugees are not to be handed over to the power of their lords, so that the lords must capture them where we live. Otherwise the people will become embittered toward us. I say to you that new developments in the present world must be very closely attended to. The old guidelines no longer function at all, for they are vain mire. As the prophet says [Ps. 75:8], 'The dregs of the cup of indignation have not yet been drained; all the wicked of the earth shall drink them. Whoever was thirsty for blood shall drink blood,' etc.

TO THE CITY COUNCIL OF NORDHAUSEN.
MÜHLHAUSEN, AFTER 15 AUGUST 1524. (#67A)[14]

May the grace and peace of God our father and our Lord, Jesus Christ, be with you.

Dearest brothers in our Lord, since you are our neighbours and, like us,[15] a free imperial city, it is not unseemly for us to open our hearts to you. We have very sorrowfully heard that the inhuman violence of [the devil] Belial has established itself among you most thirstily and with criminal violence, without any justice, in order to sacrifice the blood of Christians to Belial. This usually emerges from the hate and blindness of hardened hearts and by those who try to turn the people of God from the purity of an uncontrived faith and a knowledge of their creator. From this arises tyranny, which ruins the pure fear of God in the hearts of believers and which is the true skill of the sneaky devil – to kill the best people for the sake of the least, namely those who live for the sake of a wooden idol or image. Now this is also plainly said of you, which is not only an offence and a depravity to Christians. To turn them from the creator to crea-turely things is eternal death. Therefore, God says: 'You shall make no images; pray to, love, or tolerate no images which are made.' And notice that God forbids glorifying the sun, moon, and stars or the powers of the elements, much less the work of human hands. Those that do this shall be subject to the death sentence, as shall the prophet who teaches it.

Dearest brothers, who taught you to arrest people on account of an image? In doing this, you make clear that you defend idolatry and images – and subject yourselves to eternal death. Look, the apostle says, 'Not only those who eat but those who speak well of eating are worthy of death.' Therefore, your teacher, even if he was an angel, is damned and worthy of death. But it is obviously also Satan himself who directs you from God to the work of human hands and from pure teaching to lies. Therefore, according to the punishment of Mosaic Law, he should be stoned. It is the greatest blasphemy against God to deal with images, be it a cross or a circle, for they are wood and dead things. They cannot help themselves. Are you not ashamed of yourselves for wanting to defend saints' images because they are blessed? But your foolishness recognizes well that they are idols and cannot help themselves. Therefore, let your preacher expound Wisdom 13, 14, and 15. There you will find the meaning of blasphemy against God, so that you give the elect the eternal name of God, which is in no way stone or wood, above his name [i.e., the preacher, Süsse].

But when blasphemy occurs, then it is the adultery and whoredom about which Hosea writes [Hos. 4:2 and 4:10f.]. Just as one commits adultery outwardly against the spouse, using the sexual organs of the flesh, so adultery also occurs inwardly in the spirit if man delights in images or created things in order to mock him who is unlike all images or creatures. Thus, listen to us, in order to show the heart, with all its desires, what is right, 1 Corinthians 6[:15ff.], Romans 2[:29], Deuteronomy 10[:16], and Jeremiah 3[:17].

Hence we earnestly bid you not to put in the stocks the members [of Christ's body], redeemed through the blood of our Lord, Jesus Christ, and to release those who have been imprisoned. For it is not appropriate for Christians to kill living creatures on account of a piece of wood or an image. Man can make images, but the whole world is not able to give life to man. He who smashes an idol that blasphemes God does no injustice, for his zeal is the zeal of the Lord, and his action praises God. But you have committed an injustice and slapped God in the face much more cruelly than the heathen, John 18[:38], James 2[:25], Luke 22[:48], Matthew 26[:48ff.], and Deuteronomy 9[:6ff.].

In God's name, release the prisoners. Otherwise, you are guilty for all the blood of the just that has ever been spilled on earth – Matthew 23[:34f.], Luke 26 [see, rather, Lk. 11:49f.], and Matthew 5 – if, as you think and as is said, they have been imprisoned on account of wood and images. Release them so that God does not get angry with you. Do not sacrifice innocent blood. You do God no service with it, as you think, but rather you do it to God, Luke 9, Matthew 21. But, if you do shed blood for that reason, then you are a terrible abomination to God and to all his elect, 2 Corinthians 6, Deuteronomy 19.

May the peace of God be with you. May it sharpen your senses so that you perceive truth and justice, which the world has not received. Dear brothers, we too adhered to the abomination and the dregs of evil, but through God's grace we have been taught his truth, and to seek the highest good.

TO THE LEAGUE AT ALLSTEDT. MÜHLHAUSEN, 26 OR 27 APRIL 1525. (#75)

As a greeting, the pure fear of God [be with you], dear brothers. How long are you going to sleep? How long will you fail to acknowledge the will of God because, in your view, he has forsaken you? Oh, how often have I told you how it must be

— God cannot reveal himself otherwise. You must stand before him in resignation. If you do not do this, then the sacrifice of your heartfelt tribulation is in vain. Afterward, you have to start suffering again from the beginning. This I tell you — if you do not want to suffer for the sake of God's will, you will have to be the devil's martyrs. Therefore, guard yourselves; do not be so timid and negligent; do not flatter any longer the perverted fantasizers, the godless evildoers. Get going and fight the battle of the Lord! It is high time. Make sure that all your brothers do not mock the divine witness, otherwise they are all lost. All of Germany, France, and Italy is in motion. The master [God] wants to present his play, and now the evildoers are in for it. During Easter week, four churches belonging to religious foundations were destroyed in Fulda, the peasants in Klettgau and Hegau in the area of the Black Forest have risen, three thousand strong, and the band is getting bigger every day. My only worry is that foolish people will allow themselves to be drawn into a false compromise because as yet they do not recognize the harm [the godless have caused].

Even if there are only three of you who are firm in God and who seek only his name and honour, you need not fear a hundred thousand. Now, at them, at them, at them! It is time. The evildoers are obviously as timid as dogs. Stir up the brothers, so that they arrive at peace and give witness to their [souls'] agitation. It is infinitely, infinitely necessary. At them, at them, at them! Do not be merciful, even though Esau offers you good words, Genesis 33[:4]. Pay no heed to the lamentations of the godless. They will bid you in a friendly manner [for mercy], cry, and plead like children. Do not let yourselves be merciful, as God commanded through Moses, Deuteronomy 7[:1–5]. And God has revealed the same thing to us. Stir up the villages and cities, and especially the miners with other good fellows who would be good for our cause. We must sleep no longer.

Look, as I wrote these words, I received a message from Salza informing me how the people wanted to take the official of Duke George from the castle, because he secretly wanted to kill three of them. The peasants of the Eisfeld have taken up arms against their lords, and, shortly, they will show them no mercy. May events of this kind be an example for you. You must go at them, at them! The time is here! Balthasar and Barthel Krump, Valentin, and Bischof advance first to the dance! Pass this letter on to the miners. I have received word that my printer will come in a few days. Right now I can do nothing else. Otherwise I would give the brothers enough instruction for their hearts to become greater than all the castles and armour of the godless evildoers on earth.

At them, at them, while the fire is hot! Do not let your sword get cold, do not let your arms go lame! Strike – cling, clang! – on the anvils of Nimrod. Throw their towers to the ground! As long as [the godless] live, it is not possible for you to be emptied of human fear. You cannot be told about God as long as they rule over you. At them, at them, while you have daylight! God leads you – follow, follow! The story is already written – Matthew 24, Ezekiel 34, Daniel 74, Ezra 16, Revelation 6 – scriptural passages that are all interpreted by Romans 13.

Therefore, do not let yourselves be frightened. God is with you, as it is written in 2 Chronicles 12. God says this: 'You shall not be fearful. You shall not fear this great multitude, for it is not your fight, but rather that of the Lord. It is not you who fight there. Act bravely. You will see the hip of the Lord above you.' When Jehoshaphat heard these words, he fell down. Do likewise and through God – may he strengthen you – without fear of man and in true faith. Amen.

Dated at Mühlhausen in the year 1525.

Thomas Müntzer, a servant of God against the godless.

TO COUNT ALBRECHT OF MANSFELD.
FRANKENHAUSEN, 12 MAY 1525. (#89)[17]

Written to convert Brother Albrecht.

Fear and trembling to everyone who does evil, Romans 2[:9]. I pity the fact that you so evilly misuse the letters of Paul. Through this you want to confirm the evil authorities in all respects, just as the pope made Peter and Paul into jailers. Do you think that the lord God in his wrath cannot arouse his uncomprehending people to set aside tyrants, Hosea 13[:11] and 8[:4]? Did not the mother of Christ, speaking from the holy spirit, prophesize concerning you and your kind? Luke 1[:52]: 'He toppled the mighty from their thrones and elevated the lowly' (whom you despise). Have you not been able to find in your Lutheran grits and your Wittenberg soup what Ezekiel 37[:23,26] prophesizes? And have you not been able to taste in your Martinian manure what the same prophet says later, Ezekiel 39[:17–20], how God commands all the birds of the heavens to devour the flesh of the princes and commands the unreasoning animals to quaff the blood of the mighty ones, as is also described in the secret Revelation 18[:2–6] and 19[:17–21]? Do you think that God does not set more store on his people than on you tyrants? Under the name of Christ, you want to be a heathen, and to cloak yourself with Paul. But your way will be blocked. You may depend on that. If you want to recognize, Daniel 7[:27], that God has given power to the community, and if you want to appear before us and justify your faith, we will gladly give you this opportunity and regard you as a common brother. But if not, then we will pay no respect to your lame, insipid face, and we will fight against you as against an archenemy of the Christian faith. You may depend on that.

Written at Frankenhausen on the Friday after Jubilate [12 May] in the year 1525.

Thomas Müntzer with the sword of Gideon.

TO THE PEOPLE OF ERFURT. FRANKENHAUSEN, 13 MAY 1525. (#91)

To our dear brothers, the whole community at Erfurt.

Strength and consolation in Jesus Christ, most dearly beloved. We have heard about your steadfast love and your joyful conversion to the truth. And therefore, we want to encourage you. You will not be defeated unless the Lutheran pap-eaters have made you soft with their greased mercy, with which we have much experience. Paul says that, in our times, pleasure-seeking people cover themselves with the very best appearance of good or of pious conduct, and yet they strive both physically and verbally against the power of God. Anyone with eyes that see can easily grasp this.

Therefore it is our urgent request of you that you no longer give credence to lackeys [of the princes], and that you do not let yourselves be restrained any longer from helping common Christendom and combating with us the godless, villainous tyrants.

Help us in every way that you can, with manpower and artillery, so that we fulfil what God himself has commanded, Ezekiel 34[:25], where he says, 'I will release you from those who have beaten you with their tyranny. I will drive the wild animals from your land.' Later God says through the same prophet in Ezekiel 39[:17–20], 'Come you birds of the skies and devour the flesh of the princes, and you wild animals drink the blood of the mighty ones.' Daniel 7[:27] also says that power shall be given to the common people, Revelation 18[:2–6] and 19[:17–21]. Nearly every judgment of Scripture testifies that creatures must be free if the pure word of God is to dawn.

If you now desire truth, join with us in the circle dance that we want to dance right now, so that we faithfully repay the blasphemers of God for the dirty trick they pulled on poor Christendom. Write us back your opinion, for we are well disposed towards you, most beloved brothers.

Written at Frankenhausen on the Saturday after Jubilate [13 May] in the year of our Lord 1525.

Thomas Müntzer for the cause of common Christendom.

Notes

SPECTRES OF MÜNTZER AT SUNRISE /
GREETING THE 21ST CENTURY

1 This shouldn't surprise us: Thomas Müntzer was a collateral – but
   no less important – ancestor of today's Baptists, and many of us
   have become familiar with Baptist rhetoric through the activism of
   the Black church, the speeches of Martin Luther King, Jr, and the
   influence of that rhetoric on African American culture. Think of
   the highly imaginative talks of another radical orator, Malcolm X,
   who in his adult life chose another religion but had grown up in
   the Baptist church. Malcolm spoke out in parables (e.g., the 'house
   negro' refusing to escape from the plantation, George Washington
   bartering a slave for a barrel of molasses, etc.) and made use of
   both direct and oblique biblical references that his audience could
   easily recognize. Even his condemnation of the treacherous clergy
   reminds us of words that Müntzer uttered four centuries earlier
   and wrote in such texts as the *Prague Manifesto*.
2 'I was in Paris about two months ago [...] Let me give you a warning, if you're goin' over there, here's an example: "chapeau" means
   "hat"... "Oeuf" means "egg"... It's like those French have a different
   word for everything!', Steve Martin, *A Wild and Crazy Guy*, 1978.
3 However, bourgeois postmodernism is in the eye of the beholder,
   particularly if the beholder misses the context. While the nature
   of the novel was well comprehended in Europe, most Americans
   didn't get it. In the US – a country whose academic and literary

milieux are heavily intoxicated with metadiscourses of all kinds – Q was completely misunderstood. Some critics described the experience of reading it as precisely the opposite of what European readers had felt. Reviewing the book for the *Washington Post*, David Liss called it 'more of an anti-novel than a novel'. According to him, '*Q* gives the reader the distinct impression of purposefully exposing the clichéd conventions of the historical novel and also throwing them in the reader's face.' In the end, according to Liss, it all amounted to 'postmodern nose-thumbing'.

CHRONOLOGY OF THOMAS MÜNTZER'S LIFE

1 Adapted from Tommaso La Rocca, *Es ist Zeit. Apocalisse e storia. Studio su Thomas Müntzer*, Bologna: Cappelli, 1988.

CHAPTER I

1 Also known as the *Prague Manifesto*. The text exists in four versions: a placard-like short German version (intended for a public display that never took place), a longer German version (presented here), a Latin version, and an unfinished Czech translation. These notes rely mainly on Emidio Campi's Italian edition of Müntzer's political writings, Peter Matheson's edition of the *Collected Writings* and Hans-Jürgen Goertz's biography.
2 Jan Hus (1372–1415), Czech priest burnt at the stake as a heretic for theological positions (on indulgences, the nature of the Church, and the Eucharist) that prefigure the Reformation. Müntzer's invocation of his name is a way of calling the Czech people to revive his legacy of apostolic renewal and personal spiritual revelation against the power of the Roman Church and the stultifying use of scripture promulgated by clerics.
3 The idea that the soul must thoroughly empty itself of worldly and egoistic concerns in order to open itself up to the fear of God is a constant in Müntzer's thought, and can be related to the Christian idea of *kenosis* (cf. Paul's *Epistle to the Philippians*). The ordeal of suffering is crucial in wresting the soul away from its worldly

attachments, which is why the allegory of crucifixion and the disparaging of 'untested' souls will play such a role in his sermons and writings. The notion of mortification as a prerequisite of salvation shows the influence of mystics like Johannes Tauler (1300–1361) on Müntzer. The 'political' lesson of such a theology is that 'all relationships holding the individual in dependence on the creaturely world and diverting him from concentration on God must be abolished' (Goertz, *Thomas Müntzer*, 202).

4 This epithet possibly derives from Luther, who also linked the Church to the Babylonian tyrant.

5 Cf. Song of Songs 5:2.

6 The subordination of scripture (the 'external Bible') to spiritual revelation is a mainstay of Müntzer's thought, and a source for his defense of a plebeian Reformation against Luther's residual clericalism and authoritarianism.

7 The Biblical passage refers to the 'lying pen of the scribes' and to the 'wise' who will be shamed, in keeping with Müntzer's attack on elitist and obfuscatory uses of Scripture.

8 Asmodeus is the demon of lust in the Christian Old Testament Book of Tobit and the mediaeval demonological treatise *Malleus Maleficarum*.

9 The reference is to the *Ecclesiastical History* by Eusebius (263–339), where the Christian chronicler Hegesippus (110–180) is quoted as an authority on the early Church.

10 Cf. 2 Kings 2:15; 1 Kings 18: 18–40.

CHAPTER 2

1 The sermon was delivered on 13 July 1524 by Müntzer at the castle of Allstedt, before the Duke John of Saxony (1468–1532) and other princes. Though such sermons were customary before a preacher could officially take up his position in a parish, in Müntzer's case it was a result of the authorities' anxiety about his year and a half of activism in Allstedt, which had gained the support of the city council. Müntzer had already clashed in 1523 with his arch-enemy Count Ernst von Mansfeld and his 'League of the Elect' had participated in the iconoclastic raid on the chapel in Mallerbach.

2 Jesus' parable of the tares is to be found in Matthew 13. Müntzer alludes to it repeatedly to bring home the (concealed) presence of the godless among the true believers, and the imminence of the apocalyptic 'harvest' that will separate the wheat (the elect) from the tares (those who persist in a counterfeit faith).

3 Matheson translates this as 'taxed'.

4 Despite this rhetorical condemnation of dream interpretation, the rest of the sermon will touch repeatedly on the right use of dreams as vehicles of prophecy and spiritual illumination. Müntzer himself was beckoned to provide dream interpretation (cf. Letters #62 and 63 in *The Collected Works of Thomas Müntzer*). For Goertz, in Müntzer dreams 'become the source and the motive power of social action' (*Thomas Müntzer*, 125).

5 See note 3 to chapter 1.

6 The theme of a 'fifth empire' where coercion is mixed with extreme decadence and corruption (symbolized by the shift from gold to filth) is here translated by Müntzer into his immediate political context, in a characteristic combination of militancy and millenarianism.

7 The allusion is to the Jewish king's destruction of the idolatrous cult of Baal and the slaughter of its adherents.

CHAPTER 3

1 Begun only eighteen days after the *Sermon to the Princes*, the *Special Exposure* (or *Manifest Exposé*) signals Müntzer's irrevocable break with the princes, and contains his first remarks on the possible need for armed struggle. It comes after the repression of Müntzer sympathizers in Sangerhausen and Schönwerda, as well as in the immediate wake of the hearing in Weimar that resulted in Duke John's decree that the League of the Elect be dissolved, and that Müntzer be forbidden from preaching and publishing. Matheson notes that with the *Special Exposure* 'the power issue has become *the* issue for Müntzer', and that this 'unbelievably radical text' provides a 'structural critique and new understanding of Christian authority'.

2 The reference is to Luther's *A Letter to the Princes of Saxony Concerning the Seditious Spirit* (1524).

3 Annas was the first Roman-appointed Jewish High Priest of the province of Iudaea from AD 6 to 15. Though deposed by the Romans he was one of the priests before whom Jesus was brought for judgment.

4 Cf. Matthew 17:20: 'If ye have faith as a grain of mustard seed, ye shall say unto this mountain, Remove hence to yonder place; and it shall remove: and nothing shall be impossible unto you.'

5 The 'impossible' deification of man is a recurrent theme in Müntzer's theology.

6 A symbol of the violent power of the authorities, also used in Müntzer's correspondence (see letter #53 on page 103).

7 Caiaphas was the Jewish high priest appointed by the Romans, serving from AD 18 to 37. According to John 11:47ff. it is he who pushes the Sanhedrin to demand that Jesus be put to death, not only for blasphemy, but for proclaiming himself the Messiah.

8 See note 2 to chapter 2.

9 For Matheson, 'what they know' refers to the heathen's instinctive, natural knowledge, and what they repudiate is God's order. The juxtaposition between natural reason and spiritual revelation recurs in Müntzer's preaching.

CHAPTER 4

1 Written in a period of crisis for Müntzer (August–September 1524), which saw his exile from Allstedt, the *Highly Provoked Defence* enlists his revolutionary and apocalyptic theology, as well as his rhetorical vitriol, in a no-holds-barred retort to Luther's *A Letter to the Princes of Saxony Concerning the Seditious Spirit* (1524).

2 See the reference on page 76 to 'the clear purity of the divine law'.

3 Müntzer's correspondent John Zeiss wrote to the Duke of Saxony of a letter from Müntzer to the miners of Mansfeld, encouraging them to wash their hands in the blood of the tyrants. The letter is not extant.

4 Martin Luther, *On Trade and Usury* (1524).

5 For Müntzer's liturgical work, see *The Collected Works of Thomas Müntzer*, 162–82.

6 In Matheson's translation: 'From now on they will shit on you with a new logic, twisting the word of God.'

7 Luther advised against resistance to an article in the emperor's edict which set out that secular authorities should not interfere with punishment of married clergy, as stipulated by Canon Law.

8 A reference to Luther's 1523 hymn to two martyrs burnt in Brussels.

9 An allusion to Luther's clash with the followers of Andreas Karlstadt (1486–1541) in Orlamünde in August 1524.

10 Porcius Festus was the procurator of Iudaea before whom the apostle Paul had his final hearing.

11 A reference to the doctrine of justification by faith alone (*sola fide*), rather than works.

12 Cf. *Two Discordant and Unpleasant Imperial Edicts Concerning Luther* (1524).

13 A reference to the iconoclastic destruction of a chapel in Mallerbach (the 'goat-stall') housing a miraculous image of the Virgin Mary by followers of Müntzer from Allstedt on 24 March 1524. In his interrogation, Müntzer presents himself as a witness to what Goertz in his biography calls 'a well-considered anti-clerical action'.

14 Lawrence Süsse was an evangelical preacher in Nordhausen who, Müntzer believed, pressed Luther to write his letter to the princes. 'Unroasted' is a sarcastic reference to the martyrdom of St Lawrence on an incandescent spit.

15 Duke George of Saxony (1471–1539) would later lead the repression of the peasant revolt. Müntzer's accusation appears to have no historical basis.

16 An allusion to Luther's disputation with Johann Eck (1486–1543) in July 1519, part of which Müntzer witnessed.

17 Johann von Staupitz (1460–1524), Vicar-General of the Augustinian Order in Germany.

18 Cf. *A Sincere Admonition by Martin Luther to All Christians to Guard Against Insurrection and Rebellion* (1522).

19 In 1522 a deformed calf had been born near Freiberg; Luther refused to interpret this event 'because I am not a prophet'.

20 Luther was summoned by Emperor Charles V (1500–1558) to the Diet of Worms in April 1521 to account for his religious views. The Edict of Worms, promulgated by the emperor on 25 May 1521, branded him a heretic and forbade anyone from associating with him or his ideas.

21 Duke George of Saxony and Count Frederick von Witzleben.

22 Müntzer was summoned on 31 July 1524 before Duke John, who decreed the closure of Müntzer's printing-press and the dissolution of the League he had established with the townspeople of Allstedt and the miners of Mansfeld. Müntzer had described this covenant, this 'deterrent to the godless', as 'an emergency act of self-defence, something which is admitted by the natural judgment of all rational men' (*The Collected Works of Thomas Müntzer*, 102).

23 Müntzer fled Allstedt on the night of August 7.

CHAPTER 5

1 This implies the confession was not extorted under torture. Given the propaganda function of the text, there are doubts as to its reliability.

2 Johannes Oecolampadius (1482–1531), professor of theology at Basel, close to Zwingli, the leader of the Swiss Reformation. Ulrich Hugwald (1496–1571), Swiss humanist scholar and Anabaptist.

3 Jacob Strauss, a preacher and opponent of usury.

4 Von Gehofen had been captured by the rebels and executed in revenge for the death of one of their own. This was among the reasons for Count Ernst von Mansfeld's animus towards Müntzer.

CHAPTER 6

1 According to Matheson, this could refer to Müntzer's expulsion from his role as preacher in St George's, Halle, by the Catholic authorities after a raid by some of the people of Halle on Neuwerk monastery, in which he might have participated. Goertz suggests this is unlikely, and that the reasons for the expulsion remain unclear.

2 Matheson's translation: 'The living God is sharpening his sickle in me so that I will later be able to cut down the red poppies and the little blue flowers.'

3 A pupil of Müntzer, see his correspondence with Emmen of 3 September 1524 (letter #68).

4 Count Ernst II of Mansfeld (1479–1531) was Müntzer's main political nemesis. A convinced Catholic, he reacted with predictable irritation to Müntzer's agitation among the miners and townsfolk, as well as to Müntzer's increasingly vituperative attacks. After the rout at Frankenhausen, it was in Mansfeld's castle at Heldrungen that Müntzer was tortured and executed.

5 Frederick III, Elector of Saxony (1463–1525).

6 Müntzer is referring here to the Edict of the Imperial government of 6 March 1523.

7 Müntzer's followers in Sangerhausen, among them members of the Allstedt league, were being pressured and persecuted. Müntzer, still exercising caution, tried to restrain them while threatening the local authorities with dire consequences if they continued on this path: 'I will speak against you, sing against you, write against you, I will do the very worst that I can think up' (*The Collected Works of Thomas Müntzer*, 85).

8 A reference to the leagues, alliances or covenants that Müntzer had helped to establish.

9 Reichart (1485/6–1575) was a leading figure in the League of the Elect and in the Council of Allstedt.

10 Under the control of Frederick von Witzleben, who helped to put down the peasants' revolt.

11 A reference to Müntzer's letter to Duke John of 13 July 1524, where he pleaded for his right to print his sermons and to rebut in public the accusations against him.

12 For an account of the situation Müntzer is responding to, see Goertz, *Thomas Müntzer*, 130–31.

13 Refers either to *Counterfeit Faith* or to the *Special Exposure of False Faith*.

14 The letter is written in the first person plural, suggesting collective authorship. The manuscript copies were headed 'A writing of the rebel horde to the Nordhausen Council'.

15 The letter was sent from Mühlhausen, also an imperial city.

16 Count Albrecht von Mansfeld (1480–1560), a supporter of Luther.